Mediterranean Flavours

Cataloguing data available from Bibliothèque et Archives nationales du Québec.

03-18

Legal deposit: 2018
Bibliothèque et Archives nationales du Québec
Library and Archives Canada

ISBN 978-1-988002-86-6

Printed in Canada

EXCLUSIVE DISTRIBUTOR FOR CANADA & USA

Simon & Schuster Canada
166 King Street East, Suite 300
Toronto ON M5A 1J3

Tel: 647-427-8882
Toll Free: 800-387-0446
Fax: 647-430-9446

simonandschuster.ca
canadianliving.com/books

ART DIRECTOR Colin Elliott

EDITOR Martin Zibauer

COPY EDITOR Ruth Hanley

INDEXER Lisa Fielding

Government of Quebec – Tax credit for book publishing – Administered by SODEC. **sodec.gouv.qc.ca**

This publisher gratefully acknowledges the support of the Société de développement des enterprises culturelles du Québec.

Canada Council for the Arts Conseil des arts du Canada

We gratefully acknowledge the support of the Canada Council for the Arts for its publishing program.

We acknowledge the financial support of our publishing activity by the Government of Canada through the Canada Book Fund for our publishing activities.

Canadian Living

THE ESSENTIAL COLLECTION

Mediterranean Flavours

SIMPLE MEALS, VIBRANT FLAVOURS
125 TESTED-TILL-PERFECT RECIPES
FROM THE CANADIAN LIVING TEST KITCHEN

JUNIPER PUBLISHING
A Quebecor Media Corporation

Welcome to the Canadian Living Test Kitchen

In the Test Kitchen, we take pleasure in cooking Mediterranean-style. The foods of southern Europe, the Middle East and North Africa are simple to prepare, and the ingredients are easy to find, yet we can play with flavour combinations that are intriguing, tasty and satisfying. If that weren't enough to keep us happy, Mediterranean food—for the most part—is also healthy food. That's why we're excited to bring you this collection of recipes. Developing deliciously healthy, trustworthy recipes is the top priority for us in the Canadian Living Test Kitchen. We are recipe developers and cooks, all from different backgrounds but equally dedicated to creating great family-friendly recipes that are easy to make and successful every time.

What Does Tested Till Perfect Mean?

Every year, the food specialists in the Canadian Living Test Kitchen work together to produce approximately 500 Tested-Till-Perfect recipes. So what does Tested Till Perfect mean? It means we follow a rigorous process to ensure you'll get the same results in your kitchen as we do in ours.

Here's What We Do:

- In the Test Kitchen, we use the same everyday ingredients and equipment commonly found in kitchens across Canada.
- We start by researching ideas and brainstorming as a team.
- We write up the recipe and go straight into the kitchen to try it out.
- We taste, evaluate and tweak the recipe until we really love it.
- Once developed, each recipe gets handed off to other food specialists for more testing and another tasting session.
- We meticulously test and retest each recipe as many times as it takes to make sure it turns out as perfectly in your kitchen as it does in ours.
- We carefully weigh and measure all ingredients, record the data and send the recipe for nutritional analysis.
- The recipe is then edited and rechecked to ensure all the information is correct and it's ready for you to cook.

TESTED TILL PERFECT
Canadian Living TEST KITCHEN

Contents

Good Food, Mediterranean Style

To dieticians, eating the Mediterranean way is to follow the diet of southern Italy and Greece from the 1940s through the 1960s. To the rest of us, it means enjoying our favourite foods from the entire Mediterranean (plus Portugal, which has a similar cuisine, but an Atlantic coastline). Here, traditional meals focus on fresh vegetables, whole grains, beans and other legumes, seafood and olive oil. Yogurt and cheese are part of many meals, and desserts can be as simple as a plate of fresh fruit.

The Mediterranean diet has been linked—in highly regarded studies—to better heart health, and it's been shown to benefit people with type 2 diabetes. It's also a truly delicious way to eat. These are countries where traditional dishes are celebrated and where eating with family and friends is central to daily life. Gathering around the table and raising a glass to everyone's health are part of the Mediterranean lifestyle, too.

MEDITERRANEAN STAPLES

OLIVE OIL If it was extracted from mashed olives only by pressing or spinning, and it meets International Olive Council flavour standards, it can be called "extra-virgin." Use extra-virgin olive oil to dress salads, drizzle over vegetables or dip bread—dishes in which the oil's flavour is prominent. Trust your own palate when buying extra-virgin olive oil; taste several to find those you like and can afford.

Olive oil can lose subtle flavours when heated, so Mediterranean home cooks often save money by using olive pomace oil for frying and roasting. This blend of several grades has a neutral flavour that makes it versatile for cooking. To keep olive oil fresh, store in a sealed container away from light, humidity and heat.

FISH When you buy fish, it should smell as fresh as the open ocean. Look for bright, clear eyes—not dull, grey or cloudy—and bright red gills. Touch the flesh. It should be resilient and spring back readily. If good fresh fish is hard to get locally, don't worry. High-quality fish that's frozen on the boat can be as good as fresh, as long as you defrost it in the fridge, slowly. Don't thaw it on the counter or run it under water.

TOMATOES A perfect summer tomato smells fresh and green and has shiny, unblemished skin. Squeeze gently; it should feel firm but supple. Store fresh tomatoes at room temperature (but out of direct sunlight); tomatoes stored in the fridge lose flavour quickly and become mealy.

Mediterranean dishes often include cooked tomatoes. Roma tomatoes have fewer seeds and less moisture than other varieties, making them ideal for sauces and stews. Canned tomatoes are convenient, but brands vary in flavour, consistency and salt content; when you find one you like, stick with it. Use passata (bottled tomato purée with the seeds already strained out) when you want a smooth, seedless texture.

FRESH HERBS Many herbs, including oregano, rosemary and sage, are Mediterranean natives. Buy herbs that look fresh and green, not wilted or dry. After washing them, shake off excess water, place on a paper towel and gently roll up the towel. Refrigerate in a resealable bag or container for up to 1 week.

An easy way to use leftover fresh herbs is in one of the world's green sauces, such as Italian salsa verde, Argentinian chimichurri or English mint sauce. These simple mixes of chopped herbs, vinegar and other flavourings are quick to make, and you can improvise with herbs on hand.

LEGUMES We use a lot of canned beans in the Test Kitchen; they're the most convenient way to cook with legumes. There are differences among brands in salt content, as well as bean size and texture. If you have time to cook dried beans, you'll often give your dishes better texture and flavour, and you'll have many more options, from tiny green lentils and small brown chickpeas to giant Greek gigante beans.

Mediterranean Yogurt Dip

Mediterranean Yogurt Dip

MAKES 4 TO 6 SERVINGS
HANDS-ON TIME 5 MINUTES
TOTAL TIME 5 MINUTES

Spread 2 cups 2% Greek yogurt on large rimmed serving platter. Top with 3 tbsp prepared pesto, ¼ cup thinly sliced sun-dried tomatoes, ⅓ cup Kalamata olives, the leaves from 2 sprigs of fresh basil and 1 tbsp pine nuts. Drizzle with extra-virgin olive oil; sprinkle with hot pepper flakes, if desired.

NUTRITIONAL INFORMATION PER EACH OF 6 SERVINGS about 108 cal, 9 g pro, 6 g total fat (2 g sat. fat), 6 g carb (2 g dietary fibre, 4 g sugar), 5 mg chol, 230 mg sodium, 244 mg potassium. % RDI: 23% calcium, 5% iron, 3% vit A, 3% vit C, 1% folate.

Roasted Pepper Pomegranate Dip

MAKES ABOUT 2 CUPS
HANDS-ON TIME 5 MINUTES
TOTAL TIME 5 MINUTES

In food processor or blender, purée 1 cup chopped roasted red pepper; ½ cup chopped toasted walnuts; ½ cup toasted fresh bread crumbs; 1 jalapeño pepper, seeded and chopped; 1 tbsp pomegranate molasses; and ½ tsp each ground cumin, salt and pepper. With machine running, add 2 tbsp extra-virgin olive oil in thin steady stream. Stir in 2 cloves garlic, minced. *(Make-ahead: Refrigerate in airtight container for up to 2 days.)* Stir in 2 tbsp minced fresh parsley.

NUTRITIONAL INFORMATION PER 1 TBSP about 52 cal, 1 g pro, 4 g total fat (trace sat. fat), 3 g carb, 0 mg chol, 110 mg sodium. % RDI: 1% calcium, 2% iron, 5% vit A, 37% vit C, 4% folate.

MAKES 10 TO 12 SERVINGS
HANDS-ON TIME 20 MINUTE
TOTAL TIME 9 HOURS

Eggplant Walnut Dip
With Za'atar Pita Chips

EGGPLANT WALNUT DIP

1½ cups	whole walnuts
2	large eggplants
1	head garlic
1	can (540 mL) chickpeas, drained and rinsed
¼ cup	lemon juice
3 tbsp	tahini
1 tsp	za'atar
½ tsp	each salt and pepper
¼ tsp	cayenne pepper
½ cup	chopped fresh parsley

ZA'ATAR PITA CHIPS

6	white or whole wheat pitas
1 tbsp	vegetable oil
1 tsp	za'atar

EGGPLANT WALNUT DIP In bowl, soak walnuts in water for 8 hours; drain and pat dry. Spread on baking sheet; toast in 350°F oven, turning once, until crisp, about 15 minutes.

Using fork, prick eggplants all over; place on lightly greased baking sheet. Set aside.

Remove 1 clove garlic from head; peel, mince and set aside. Slice off top third of remaining garlic head to expose cloves; wrap in foil and add to baking sheet. Bake in 375°F oven, turning eggplants once, until soft, 40 to 45 minutes. Let stand until eggplants are cool enough to handle.

Cut eggplants in half lengthwise; using spoon, scoop flesh into food processor. Squeeze cloves of roasted garlic from skins into food processor. Add chickpeas; pulse until combined.

Add walnuts, lemon juice, tahini, za'atar, reserved minced garlic, salt, pepper and cayenne pepper; pulse until walnuts are finely chopped. Stir in parsley. Cover and refrigerate for 1 hour. *(Make-ahead: Cover and refrigerate for up to 2 days.)*

ZA'ATAR PITA CHIPS Brush 1 side of each pita with oil; sprinkle with za'atar. Cut each into 8 wedges; arrange on baking sheet. Bake in 350°F oven until crisp, about 8 minutes. *(Make-ahead: Let cool; store in airtight container for up to 2 days.)* Serve with dip.

NUTRITIONAL INFORMATION PER EACH OF 12 SERVINGS about 278 cal, 8 g pro, 12 g total fat (1 g sat. fat), 37 g carb (6 g dietary fibre, 5 g sugar), 0 mg chol, 357 mg sodium, 305 mg potassium. % RDI: 8% calcium, 18% iron, 3% vit A, 13% vit C, 34% folate.

TIP FROM THE TEST KITCHEN

Za'atar is a Middle Eastern herb blend that usually includes ground sesame seeds, thyme, sumac, marjoram and oregano. It's available in many grocery stores.

Soaking the walnuts overnight gets rid of the astringency that some people dislike.

Roasted Sweet Potato Hummus

MAKES 3 CUPS
HANDS-ON TIME 10 MINUTES
TOTAL TIME 4½ HOURS

2 cups	diced peeled sweet potato (about 1 large)
3 tbsp	olive oil
1	can (540 mL) chickpeas, drained
¼ cup	tahini
3 tbsp	lemon juice
3	cloves garlic, pressed or finely grated
1 tsp	salt

Toss sweet potato with 1 tbsp of the oil. Arrange in single layer on parchment paper–lined baking sheet; bake in 400°F oven until browned and tender, 15 to 20 minutes. Let cool.

In food processor, purée together chickpeas, tahini, lemon juice, garlic, remaining oil, the salt, ¼ cup water and sweet potato until smooth. Transfer to bowl; refrigerate until cooled, about 4 hours. Stir to loosen before serving.

NUTRITIONAL INFORMATION PER ¼ CUP about 128 cal, 3 g pro, 7 g total fat (1 g sat. fat), 15 g carb (3 g dietary fibre, 3 g sugar), 0 mg chol, 302 mg sodium, 151 mg potassium. % RDI: 4% calcium, 8% iron, 46% vit A, 10% vit C, 13% folate.

TIP FROM THE TEST KITCHEN

If you're pressed for time, you can take a kitchen shortcut by starting with store-bought hummus. In blender, purée together cooked sweet potato and hummus.

MAKES 6 TO 8 SERVINGS
HANDS-ON TIME 15 MINUTES
TOTAL TIME 15 MINUTES

Creamy Feta Dip
With Lemon-Oregano Shrimp

CREAMY FETA DIP

1 cup crumbled feta cheese
1 small clove garlic, minced
⅔ cup light sour cream
⅓ cup light mayonnaise
¼ tsp grated lemon zest
2 tsp lemon juice
1 tbsp chopped fresh chives

LEMON-OREGANO SHRIMP

2 tsp olive oil
2 cloves garlic, minced
¼ tsp Italian herb seasoning
450 g large shrimp (21 to 24 count), peeled and deveined
pinch salt
1 tbsp chopped fresh oregano
2 tsp lemon juice

CREAMY FETA DIP In food processor, blend feta with garlic until smooth. Add sour cream, mayonnaise, lemon zest and lemon juice; blend until smooth. Transfer to bowl; stir in chives.

LEMON-OREGANO SHRIMP In large nonstick skillet, heat oil over medium heat; cook garlic and Italian seasoning, stirring often, until fragrant, about 1 minute. Add shrimp and salt; cook, stirring occasionally, until shrimp are pink and opaque throughout, about 4 minutes. Stir in oregano and lemon juice. Serve with feta dip.

NUTRITIONAL INFORMATION PER EACH OF 8 SERVINGS about 174 cal, 13 g pro, 12 g total fat (5 g sat. fat), 4 g carb (trace dietary fibre, 1 g sugar), 100 mg chol, 362 mg sodium, 160 mg potassium. % RDI: 14% calcium, 10% iron, 7% vit A, 5% vit C, 6% folate.

TIP FROM THE TEST KITCHEN

In the Test Kitchen, even when shrimp is labelled as deveined, we take a quick look at each one to be sure it's been cleaned adequately. If we're buying frozen shrimp, we prefer uncooked, which has better texture and flavour than cooked. Shrimp cooks so quickly, there's no time saved by buying frozen cooked shrimp.

Homemade Ricotta Cheese

MAKES ABOUT 2 CUPS
HANDS-ON TIME 20 MINUTES
TOTAL TIME 1½ HOURS

8 cups homogenized milk
½ tsp salt
⅓ cup white vinegar

In large heavy-bottomed saucepan, heat milk with salt over low heat, stirring often, until instant-read thermometer reads 203°F, about 40 minutes.

Add vinegar; slowly stir 3 times. Remove from heat. Let stand for 20 minutes.

Line fine-mesh sieve with 2 layers of damp cheesecloth. Using slotted spoon, gently skim off curds and place in sieve. Let drain for 30 minutes. Transfer to serving bowl.

NUTRITIONAL INFORMATION PER TBSP about 25 cal, 2 g pro, 2 g total fat (1 g sat. fat), 1 g carb (trace dietary fibre), 7 mg chol, 19 mg sodium, 18 mg potassium. % RDI: 5% calcium, 1% vit A, 1% folate.

SERVE WITH

Crostini & Toppings

Broil ½-inch thick slices of baguette or other crusty bread until crisp and golden, about 2 minutes per side. Spread with ricotta. Top with any of these suggested combinations:

- crushed roasted hazelnuts and liquid honey
- grilled peaches and prosciutto
- roasted cherry tomatoes, balsamic vinegar and fresh basil
- fig slices, baby arugula and cracked pepper

MAKES 4 CUPS
HANDS-ON TIME 15 MINUTES
TOTAL TIME 25 MINUTES

Warm Olives & Chorizo

2 tbsp	extra-virgin olive oil
125 g	smoked chorizo or other smoked sausage, thinly sliced
1 cup	unpitted brined black olives (such as Kalamata)
1 cup	unpitted oil-cured black olives
1 cup	unpitted large green olives
2	cloves garlic, thinly sliced
1 tsp	hot pepper flakes
half	small navel orange, thinly sliced crosswise
1 tbsp	fresh sage leaves, thinly sliced

In large skillet, heat oil over medium heat; cook chorizo, stirring, for 1 minute.

Add brined black olives, oil-cured black olives, green olives, garlic and hot pepper flakes; cook, stirring occasionally, until heated through and fragrant, about 3 minutes.

Stir in orange and sage; cook until orange begins to break down, about 2 minutes. Remove from heat; cover and let stand for 10 minutes. Serve warm. *(Make-ahead: Cover and refrigerate for up to 3 days; reheat before serving.)*

NUTRITIONAL INFORMATION PER 2 TBSP about 61 cal, 1 g pro, 6 g total fat (1 g sat. fat), 2 g carb (1 g dietary fibre), 3 mg chol, 393 mg sodium, 27 mg potassium. % RDI: 1% calcium, 1% iron, 1% vit A, 3% vit C.

MAKES ABOUT 2½ CUPS
HANDS-ON TIME 4 MINUTES
TOTAL TIME 8 MINUTES

Black Olive Spread

375 g	oil-cured black olives
¼ cup	extra-virgin olive oil
1 tbsp	red wine vinegar
2 tsp	dried thyme
pinch	hot pepper flakes
2	cloves garlic, minced
3	capers

Soak olives in cold water for 5 minutes; drain and pat dry. Pit olives.

In food processor, pulse together olives, oil, vinegar, thyme and hot pepper flakes until finely chopped. Scrape into serving bowl. *(Make-ahead: Cover and refrigerate for up to 5 days.)* Stir in garlic; garnish with capers.

NUTRITIONAL INFORMATION PER 1 TBSP about 42 cal, trace pro, 4 g total fat (trace sat. fat), 1 g carb, 0 mg chol, 397 mg sodium. % RDI: 1% calcium, 2% iron.

Golden Gazpacho Shooters

MAKES 8 SERVINGS
HANDS-ON TIME 20 MINUTES
TOTAL TIME 24½ HOURS

450 g	yellow cherry tomatoes, halved
1	sweet yellow pepper, chopped
½ cup	chopped sweet onion
½ cup	chopped peeled English cucumber
1	small clove garlic
1 tbsp	finely chopped fresh cilantro
2 tsp	lemon juice
1½ tsp	white wine vinegar
1 tsp	Worcestershire sauce
¼ tsp	each salt and pepper
quarter	large avocado

In blender, coarsely purée tomatoes. Add yellow pepper, onion, cucumber and garlic; purée until smooth. Using spatula, press through fine-mesh sieve into bowl, occasionally scraping purée from underside of sieve with spoon.

Stir in cilantro, lemon juice, vinegar, Worcestershire sauce, salt and pepper. Refrigerate in airtight container for 24 hours.

Divide among 8 small glasses. Peel and thinly slice avocado lengthwise; add to glasses as garnish.

NUTRITIONAL INFORMATION PER SERVING about 29 cal, 1 g pro, 1 g total fat (trace sat. fat), 5 g carb (1 g dietary fibre, 2 g sugar), 0 mg chol, 94 mg sodium, 243 mg potassium. % RDI: 1% calcium, 4% iron, 1% vit A, 58% vit C, 13% folate.

TIP FROM THE TEST KITCHEN

Letting this soup rest in the fridge for about 24 hours mellows the onion and garlic flavours. The soup will separate, but a gentle stir brings it back together.

MAKES ABOUT 42 PIECES
HANDS-ON TIME 20 MINUTES
TOTAL TIME 37 HOURS

Spanish Salt Cod Fritters

1	pkg (400 g) bone-in salt cod
675 g	russet potatoes, peeled and quartered
3 tbsp	extra-virgin olive oil
¼ cup	all-purpose flour
3	large eggs
⅓ cup	finely chopped green onion
⅓ cup	chopped fresh parsley
1 clove	garlic, minced
¼ tsp	pepper
	vegetable oil for deep-frying

Cut fish into 4 pieces; rinse well with cold water. In large deep bowl, soak in cold water in refrigerator for 36 hours, changing water 4 times. Taste fish; if still too salty, continue changing water and soaking for up to 8 hours longer. Drain and rinse.

In saucepan, cover fish with cold water and bring to simmer over medium-high heat. Turn off heat; let stand until fish flakes easily when tested, about 20 minutes. Reserving water, drain well; let cool. Remove and discard skin and bones; flake fish. Set aside.

In saucepan of reserved water, boil potatoes until tender, about 15 minutes; drain well. Return to pan over medium-low heat to dry for 30 seconds; mash. Transfer to bowl.

In clean saucepan, bring ¾ cup water and the olive oil to boil over medium heat; vigorously whisk in flour until smooth, about 2 minutes. Remove from heat. Whisk for 1 minute. Whisk in eggs, 1 at a time.

Stir in potatoes, green onions, parsley, garlic and pepper. Stir in fish just until incorporated; let cool.

In Dutch oven or heavy-bottomed saucepan, add enough oil to come 2 inches up side. Heat until deep-fryer thermometer reads 375°F. Drop fish mixture by heaping 1 tbsp into hot oil; deep-fry, turning once, until golden brown, 4 to 5 minutes. Using slotted spatula, transfer to paper towel–lined tray to drain.

NUTRITIONAL INFORMATION PER PIECE about 114 cal, 6 g pro, 9 g total fat (1 g sat. fat), 3 g carb (0 g dietary fibre, 0 g sugar), 25 mg chol, 583 mg sodium, 159 mg potassium. % RDI: 2% calcium, 3% iron, 1% vit A, 3% vit C, 3% folate.

Egyptian-Style Fava Falafels

MAKES ABOUT 28 PIECES
HANDS-ON TIME 25 MINUTES
TOTAL TIME 24½ HOURS

2 cups	dried shelled fava beans
3 tbsp	coriander seeds
1 tbsp	cumin seeds
1	onion
6	cloves garlic, minced
1¼ cups	packed fresh coriander leaf and stems
1 cup	packed fresh parsley leaves
1½ tsp	sea salt
1½ tsp	kosher salt
pinch	cayenne pepper (optional)
½ tsp	sesame seeds
	vegetable oil for deep-frying

Soak fava beans in water for 24 hours; drain and rinse. In food processor, pulse beans until in coarse meal. Transfer to large bowl; set aside.

In skillet, toast coriander seeds over medium-low heat, stirring, until slightly darkened, 1 to 2 minutes. Add cumin seeds; toast until darkened, 30 seconds. Let cool. Using spice grinder or clean coffee grinder, grind seeds. Add to beans.

In food processor, purée onion, garlic, fresh coriander and parsley. Add to beans along with salt, and cayenne pepper (if using). *(Make-ahead: Freeze in airtight container for up to 1 month.)*

Form by 2 tbsp into balls. Using thumb, press sesame seeds into centre of each to form 2-inch rounds.

In Dutch oven or heavy-bottomed saucepan, add enough oil to come ½ inch up side. Heat until deep-fryer thermometer reads 350°F. Deep-fry falafels, working in batches and turning once, until darkened, 2 to 3 minutes. Using slotted spatula, transfer to paper towel–lined tray to drain.

NUTRITIONAL INFORMATION PER PIECE about 159 cal, 4 g pro, 12 g total fat (1 g sat. fat), 10 g carb (0 g dietary fibre), 0 mg chol, 143 mg sodium, 162 mg potassium. % RDI: 3% calcium, 9% iron, 3% vit A, 10% vit C, 21% folate.

SERVE WITH

Spiced Tahini Sauce

In small bowl, combine ⅔ cup tahini; ⅓ cup lemon juice; 1 clove garlic, minced; 3 tbsp minced fresh parsley; ½ tsp each salt and paprika; and ¼ tsp each cayenne pepper and ground cumin. Slowly mix in ¼ cup cold water until thick pouring consistency, thinning with more water if desired.

MAKES 12 SERVINGS
HANDS-ON TIME 15 MINUTES
TOTAL TIME 35 MINUTES

Grilled Antipasto Focaccia Sandwich

1	loaf rosemary focaccia
2	roasted red peppers, finely chopped and patted dry
1	tomato, thinly sliced
100 g	sliced Calabrese salami or soppressata (about 16 slices), julienned
⅓ cup	coarsely chopped green olives
225 g	fresh mozzarella cheese, drained and sliced
¼ cup	basil leaves, torn

Split focaccia lengthwise. Arrange red peppers, tomato, salami, olives, mozzarella and basil on bottom half.

Sandwich with top half; wrap well in foil and place on grill. Place cast-iron skillet or brick wrapped in foil over top. Close lid and grill over medium heat, turning once, until warmed through and mozzarella is melted, 12 to 14 minutes. Let stand for 5 minutes before slicing.

NUTRITIONAL INFORMATION PER SERVING about 200 cal, 9 g pro, 9 g total fat (4 g sat. fat), 21 g carb (2 g dietary fibre, 1 g sugar), 22 mg chol, 465 mg sodium, 86 mg potassium. % RDI: 10% calcium, 148% iron, 10% vit A, 48% vit C, 18% folate.

TIP FROM THE TEST KITCHEN

Loaf-style sandwiches are great for family buffets and casual parties: serve on a wooden board with a serrated knife, and everyone can slice off as much or as little as they like.

The Ultimate Pizza Dough

MAKES ONE 8-SLICE CRUST
HANDS-ON TIME 15 MINUTES
TOTAL TIME 24¼ HOURS

2 cups	all-purpose flour (approx)
1 tsp	quick-rising (instant) dry yeast
½ tsp	salt
⅔ cup	warm water
2 tsp	olive oil

In large bowl, whisk together 1½ cups of the flour, the yeast and salt. Using wooden spoon, stir in warm water and olive oil until ragged dough forms.

Turn out onto lightly floured surface; knead dough, adding as much of the remaining flour, a little at a time, as needed to make smooth, elastic dough (slightly tacky to the touch, but won't stick to hands or work surface), about 8 minutes.

Transfer to greased bowl; turn dough to grease all over. Cover with plastic wrap. Refrigerate for 24 hours (or let rise in warm, draft-free place until doubled in bulk, about 1½ hours).

To make regular pizza: On lightly floured surface, roll out dough into 12-inch circle; transfer to greased pizza pan. Add desired toppings. Bake on bottom rack in 500°F oven until crust is golden, 12 to 15 minutes.

To make thin-crust pizza: On lightly floured surface, roll out dough into 14-inch circle; transfer to greased pizza pan. Add desired toppings. Bake on bottom rack in 500°F oven until crust is golden, 12 to 15 minutes.

NUTRITIONAL INFORMATION PER EACH OF 8 SLICES (WITHOUT TOPPINGS) about 125 cal, 4 g pro, 2 g total fat (trace sat. fat), 23 g carb (1 g dietary fibre, trace sugar), 0 mg chol, 144 mg sodium, 40 mg potassium. % RDI: 1% calcium, 11% iron, 23% folate.

TIP FROM THE TEST KITCHEN

It's hard to resist, but try not to overload a pizza with toppings, especially if you like a crisp thin crust. If there's too much good stuff on top, the crust may be cooked long before the toppings.

MAKES 8 TO 10 SLICES
HANDS-ON TIME 20 MINUTES
TOTAL TIME 1¾ HOURS

Fresh Tomato Pizza
With Basil-Garlic Sauce

675 g	tomatoes, cut in scant ½-inch thick rounds
½ tsp	salt
1 cup	packed fresh basil leaves
¼ cup	extra-virgin olive oil
3	cloves garlic, smashed
pinch	pepper
pinch	hot pepper flakes (optional)
¼ cup	finely grated Parmesan cheese
	prepared pizza dough (670 to 750 g)
200 g	fresh mozzarella cheese, drained and sliced

In colander over bowl, layer tomatoes; sprinkle with ¼ tsp of the salt. Let stand for 1 hour. Using palms of hands, gently press out excess liquid; set tomatoes aside.

Meanwhile, in food processor, purée basil, oil, garlic, pepper, hot pepper flakes (if using) and remaining salt. Stir in Parmesan.

On lightly floured work surface, shape dough into 14-inch round by pressing with fingertips and pulling at edge to stretch. Transfer to parchment paper–lined pizza pan. Spread basil sauce over surface; top with tomatoes.

Bake on bottom rack of 450°F oven until bottom of crust is golden, 15 to 17 minutes. Top with mozzarella; bake until melted, about 3 minutes.

NUTRITIONAL INFORMATION PER EACH OF 10 SLICES about 300 cal, 10 g pro, 15 g total fat (5 g sat. fat), 32 g carb (2 g dietary fibre, 4 g sugar), 18 mg chol, 430 mg sodium, 148 mg potassium. % RDI: 19% calcium, 15% iron, 6% vit A, 5% vit C, 29% folate.

TIP FROM THE TEST KITCHEN

Lightly salting the tomatoes and gently pressing out excess liquid improves their texture and helps avoid a soggy crust.

If the dough tends to spring back to its original shape after stretching, give it a few minutes to relax.

Turkish Roast Lamb Pizza

MAKES 4 TO 6 SERVINGS
HANDS-ON TIME 45 MINUTES
TOTAL TIME 1 HOUR

CREAMY GARLIC SAUCE In small bowl, whisk together yogurt, mayonnaise, oil, garlic, salt and pepper. Set aside. *(Make-ahead: Refrigerate in airtight container for up to 3 days.)*

PIZZA In saucepan, heat oil over medium heat; cook onion, red pepper and garlic, stirring often, until softened and onions are lightly browned, 8 to 10 minutes. Add tomatoes, salt, pepper and 3 tbsp water; cook, stirring occasionally, until tomatoes are broken down and mixture is slightly thickened, 12 to 15 minutes. Remove from heat; let cool.

Divide dough in half. On lightly floured work surface, shape each half into 18- x 6-inch oval by pressing with fingertips and pulling at edge to stretch. Transfer to greased large baking sheet. Spread tomato mixture over crusts; sprinkle with lamb.

Bake on bottom rack of 475°F oven, rotating sheet halfway through, until dough is puffed and golden, 15 to 18 minutes. Drizzle with garlic sauce and sprinkle with mint.

NUTRITIONAL INFORMATION PER EACH OF 6 SERVINGS about 521 cal, 23 g pro, 22 g total fat (6 g sat. fat), 55 g carb (4 g dietary fibre, 8 g sugar), 39 mg chol, 683 mg sodium, 472 mg potassium. % RDI: 14% calcium, 34% iron, 11% vit A, 57% vit C, 56% folate.

CREAMY GARLIC SAUCE

- **¼ cup** Balkan-style yogurt
- **2 tbsp** light mayonnaise
- **2 tsp** olive oil
- **1** small clove garlic, pressed or finely grated
- **pinch** each salt and pepper

PIZZA

- **2 tbsp** olive oil
- **1** onion, finely diced
- **half** sweet red pepper, finely diced
- **2** cloves garlic, minced
- **2** plum tomatoes, seeded and diced
- **¼ tsp** each salt and pepper
- **650 g** prepared pizza dough
- **2 cups** diced cooked roast lamb
- **⅓ cup** torn fresh mint

MAKES 32 PIECES
HANDS-ON TIME 35 MINUTES
TOTAL TIME 1¼ HOURS

Spinach & Artichoke Pissaladière

1 tbsp	butter
1	sweet onion, thinly sliced
1 tbsp	red wine vinegar
pinch	each salt and pepper
2	sheets (450 g pkg) frozen butter puff pastry, thawed
½ cup	water-packed artichoke hearts (about 2), drained, chopped and patted dry
¼ cup	thinly sliced drained oil-packed sun-dried tomatoes
3 cups	lightly packed baby spinach, thinly sliced

In skillet, melt butter over medium heat; cook onion, stirring occasionally, until softened and golden, about 20 minutes. Stir in vinegar, salt and pepper.

On parchment paper–lined rimless baking sheet, unroll 1 sheet of the pastry. Top with half each of the onion mixture, artichokes, sun-dried tomatoes and spinach. On separate baking sheet, repeat with remaining pastry, onion mixture, artichokes, sun-dried tomatoes and spinach. Bake, 1 sheet at time, in 425°F oven until edges are golden, 18 to 20 minutes. Cut each sheet into 16 squares.

NUTRITIONAL INFORMATION PER PIECE about 71 cal, 1 g pro, 4 g total fat (2 g sat. fat), 7 g carb (1 g dietary fibre, 1 g sugar), 7 mg chol, 63 mg sodium, 61 mg potassium. % RDI: 1% calcium, 4% iron, 5% vit A, 5% vit C, 4% folate.

TIP FROM THE TEST KITCHEN

After 20 minutes in the skillet, the onion slices will be soft and a little sticky. They should be evenly coloured without any burnt bits. If they begin to stick to the pan, add up to 1 tbsp water, a little at a time.

Spinach & Feta Burek

MAKES 64 PIECES
HANDS-ON TIME 1 HOUR
TOTAL TIME 1½ HOURS

1	pkg (284 g) spinach, trimmed
375 g	feta cheese, crumbled
1	pkg (250 g) cream cheese, softened
1	large egg
2 tbsp	chopped fresh dill
1½ tsp	grated lemon zest
1	clove garlic, minced
½ tsp	each salt and pepper
¼ tsp	ground allspice
16	sheets phyllo pastry
¾ cup	butter, melted

In steamer basket set over saucepan of simmering water, steam spinach until wilted. Using back of spoon, press out and discard liquid; coarsely chop spinach. Set aside.

In bowl, beat feta with cream cheese until light and fluffy. Beat in egg, dill, lemon zest, garlic, salt, pepper and allspice. Stir in spinach.

Place 1 phyllo sheet on work surface, keeping remainder covered with damp towel (to prevent drying out). Brush lightly with butter.

Cut lengthwise to make four 2½-inch wide strips; discard remaining strip.

Spoon 1 tbsp of the spinach mixture ½ inch from end of 1 strip. Fold 1 corner of phyllo over filling so bottom edge of phyllo meets side edge to form triangle. Continue folding triangle sideways and upward until end of strip; fold end flap over to adhere. Repeat with remaining phyllo and spinach mixture.

Brush both sides of triangles with remaining butter. *(Make-ahead: Layer between waxed paper in airtight container; freeze for up to 2 weeks. Bake from frozen.)* Bake on baking sheet in 375°F oven until golden, about 18 minutes.

NUTRITIONAL INFORMATION PER PIECE: about 67 cal, 2 g pro, 5 g total fat (3 g sat. fat), 4 g carb (trace dietary fibre), 18 mg chol, 137 mg sodium, 33 mg potassium. % RDI: 3% calcium, 3% iron, 8% vit A, 6% folate.

MAKES 16 SERVINGS
HANDS-ON TIME 30 MINUTES
TOTAL TIME 2½ HOURS

Asiago & Fennel Grissini
With Prosciutto

½ tsp	granulated sugar
⅓ cup	warm water
½ tsp	active dry yeast
1 cup	all-purpose flour (approx)
½ cup	finely shredded Asiago or Parmesan cheese
1 tsp	fennel seeds
¼ tsp	salt
¼ tsp	hot pepper flakes
3 tbsp	extra-virgin olive oil
16	slices prosciutto
⅔ cup	packed baby arugula

In liquid measure, stir sugar with water until dissolved; sprinkle yeast over top. Let stand until frothy, about 10 minutes.

In bowl, stir together flour, Asiago, fennel seeds, salt and hot pepper flakes; stir in 2 tbsp of the oil. Stir in yeast mixture to form ragged dough.

Turn out onto lightly floured work surface; knead until smooth and elastic, dusting with more flour as necessary, 2 to 3 minutes. Place dough in greased bowl, turning to grease all over. Cover with plastic wrap; let rise in warm draft-free place until doubled in size, about 1½ hours.

Punch down dough. Turn out onto lightly floured work surface; divide into 16 pieces. Using fingertips, roll each piece into 10-inch long rope. Arrange on parchment paper–lined baking sheet. Brush with remaining oil.

Bake in 375°F oven, rotating halfway through, until edges are crisp and golden, 12 to 15 minutes. Let cool to room temperature.

Separate prosciutto slices. Working with 1 slice at a time, arrange a few arugula leaves over top; place tip of breadstick on top and roll prosciutto around breadstick, enclosing arugula. Repeat with remaining breadsticks, prosciutto and arugula.

NUTRITIONAL INFORMATION PER SERVING about 90 cal, 5 g pro, 5 g total fat (1 g sat. fat), 6 g carb (0 g dietary fibre, 0 g sugar), 15 mg chol, 344 mg sodium, 90 mg potassium. % RDI: 3% calcium, 4% iron, 1% vit A, 7% folate.

Ginger Orange Steaks
With Apricot Couscous

MAKES 4 SERVINGS
HANDS-ON TIME 25 MINUTES
TOTAL TIME 30 MINUTES

GINGER ORANGE STEAKS

4	beef top sirloin grilling steak medallions (each about 150 g)
pinch	salt and pepper
2 tbsp	olive oil
2	cloves garlic
2 tsp	fresh ginger
¾ cup	sodium-reduced beef broth
⅓ cup	orange juice
1 tsp	Dijon mustard

APRICOT COUSCOUS

1½ cups	sodium-reduced beef broth
2 cups	frozen broccoli florets
1 cup	couscous
¼ cup	diced dried apricots
¼ tsp	each salt and pepper

GINGER ORANGE STEAKS Sprinkle steaks with salt and pepper. In Dutch oven or large heavy-bottomed saucepan, heat half of the oil over medium heat; cook steaks, turning once, until medium-rare, 8 to 10 minutes. Transfer to plate; tent with foil to keep warm.

In same pan, heat remaining oil over medium heat; cook garlic and ginger, stirring, until fragrant, about 30 seconds. Add broth, orange juice and mustard, stirring up browned bits; bring to boil. Reduce heat and simmer, stirring occasionally, until reduced by half, about 5 minutes. Scrape into serving dish; keep warm. Drizzle over steaks before serving.

APRICOT COUSCOUS In same pan, bring broth to boil. Add broccoli; cook, stirring, for 1 minute. Remove from heat; stir in couscous, apricots, salt and pepper. Cover and let stand until liquid is absorbed, about 5 minutes. Fluff with fork; serve with steaks.

NUTRITIONAL INFORMATION PER SERVING about 465 cal, 31 g pro, 16 g total fat (4 g sat. fat), 50 g carb (4 g dietary fibre, 15 g sugar), 55 mg chol, 583 mg sodium, 787 mg potassium. % RDI: 7% calcium, 26% iron, 11% vit A, 102% vit C, 32% folate.

TIP FROM THE TEST KITCHEN

Couscous grains are tiny balls of steamed and dried durum semolina. Couscous is usually considered a pasta, although it's prepared more like a grain. For an easy fibre boost, use whole wheat couscous; it cooks just as quickly as the regular kind.

MAKES 4 TO 6 SERVINGS
HANDS-ON TIME 30 MINUTES
TOTAL TIME 45 MINUTES

T-Bone Steak Florentine

1 kg	beef T-bone grilling steak (1½ inches thick)
2 tsp	olive oil
1 tsp	chopped fresh rosemary
¾ tsp	fine sea salt
½ tsp	pepper
	lemon wedges

Brush both sides of steak with oil and sprinkle with rosemary. Let stand for 10 minutes.

Sprinkle both sides of steak with salt and pepper, pressing to adhere. Place on greased grill over medium-high heat. Leave lid open and grill, rotating in quarter-turns and turning as necessary to prevent overbrowning, until instant-read thermometer inserted in centre reads 125°F, 18 to 20 minutes. Using tongs, stand steak up on base of T-bone and grill until instant-read thermometer inserted in centre reads 130°F, about 4 minutes.

Transfer to rack and let stand, uncovered, for 5 minutes or until instant-read thermometer inserted in centre reads 135°F. Slice across the grain and serve with lemon wedges.

NUTRITIONAL INFORMATION PER EACH OF 6 SERVINGS about 273 cal, 28 g pro, 17 g total fat (7 g sat. fat), trace carb (trace dietary fibre, 0 g sugar), 66 mg chol, 350 mg sodium, 302 mg potassium. % RDI: 2% calcium, 19% iron, 3% folate.

TIP FROM THE TEST KITCHEN

T-bone steaks have two parts, separated by the bone: the smaller, leaner tenderloin side and the larger, fattier strip loin. The tenderloin piece cooks slightly faster, so serve it to those who prefer a steak that is a bit more done.

Beef Vegetable Stew
With Prunes & Apricots

MAKES 10 SERVINGS
HANDS-ON TIME 35 MINUTES
TOTAL TIME 3 HOURS

1 tbsp	vegetable oil
2	onions, thinly sliced
2	stalks celery, thinly sliced
1.35 kg	stewing beef cubes
½ tsp	each salt and pepper
2	cloves garlic, minced
2 tsp	ground ginger
½ tsp	each cinnamon and ground allspice
2	bay leaves
3 cups	sodium-reduced beef broth
1 cup	dry red wine
⅓ cup	cider vinegar
2 tbsp	packed brown sugar
2 tsp	Worcestershire sauce
4	carrots, chopped
2	white turnips, peeled and cubed
½ cup	pitted prunes, chopped
½ cup	dried apricots, chopped
2 tbsp	all-purpose flour
2 tbsp	cold water

In Dutch oven or large heavy-bottomed saucepan, heat 1 tsp of the oil over medium heat; cook onions and celery, stirring occasionally, until softened, about 7 minutes. Scrape into bowl.

Toss together beef, salt and pepper. Add remaining oil to pan; heat over medium-high heat. Cook beef, in batches and stirring occasionally, until browned, about 6 minutes. Stir in garlic; cook, stirring, until fragrant, about 1 minute.

Add onion mixture, ginger, cinnamon, allspice and bay leaves; cook, stirring, for 1 minute. Stir in broth, wine, vinegar, brown sugar and Worcestershire sauce; bring to boil. Reduce heat, cover and simmer for 1½ hours.

Stir in carrots, turnips, prunes and apricots; cook, stirring occasionally, until turnips are tender, about 45 minutes. Discard bay leaves.

Whisk flour with cold water; whisk into stew. Simmer until slightly thickened, about 10 minutes. *(Make-ahead: Let cool for 30 minutes. Refrigerate in airtight container for up to 3 days or freeze for up to 1 month.)*

NUTRITIONAL INFORMATION PER SERVING about 341 cal, 29 g pro, 15 g total fat (6 g sat. fat), 22 g carb (3 g dietary fibre, 13 g sugar), 80 mg chol, 452 mg sodium, 778 mg potassium. % RDI: 6% calcium, 26% iron, 54% vit A, 13% vit C, 10% folate.

MAKES 8 TO 10 SERVINGS
HANDS-ON TIME 45 MINUTES
TOTAL TIME 4¼ HOURS

Hearty Italian Pot Roast

2 tbsp	olive oil
2	cross rib or blade pot roasts (each 1.5 to 1.7 kg)
6	cloves garlic, smashed
2	bay leaves
1	red onion, quartered
2	carrots, halved crosswise
2	stalks celery, halved crosswise
2 tsp	fennel seeds
1½ tbsp	cocoa powder
5	sprigs fresh rosemary
1	pkg (14 g) dried wild mushrooms, coarsely torn
1½ cups	red wine
1	pkg (900 mL) sodium-reduced beef broth
1	can (796 mL) whole plum tomatoes, coarsely crushed
3 tbsp	cornstarch

In Dutch oven or large heavy-bottomed saucepan, heat 1 tbsp of the oil over medium-high heat; working in batches, cook beef, turning occasionally until browned all over, 3 to 5 minutes. Transfer to 16- x 12-inch roasting pan; set aside.

Reduce heat to medium. Add remaining oil to Dutch oven; cover and cook garlic, bay leaves, red onion, carrots, celery and fennel seeds, stirring occasionally, until softened, about 8 minutes. Increase heat to medium-high; stir in cocoa powder, rosemary and mushrooms. Add wine; cook, scraping up any browned bits, for 5 minutes. Stir in broth and tomatoes (including juices); bring to boil. Transfer tomato mixture to roasting pan.

Cover with foil; braise in 325°F oven, turning beef twice, until fork-tender, about 3½ hours.

Transfer beef to cutting board. Remove any twine; slice beef across grain, trimming excess fat. Keep warm.

Skim fat from surface of cooking liquid. Strain cooking liquid and vegetables through fine-mesh sieve into large saucepan. Using metal or wooden spoon, press down on vegetables to extract liquid; discard vegetables.

Place pan over medium-high heat; bring to boil. In small bowl, whisk cornstarch with 3 tbsp water; whisk into pan. Simmer, stirring often, until thickened, about 3 minutes. Serve with beef.

NUTRITIONAL INFORMATION PER EACH OF 10 SERVINGS about 220 cal, 31 g pro, 8 g total fat (3 g sat. fat), 7 g carb (1 g dietary fibre, 3 g sugar), 67 mg chol, 267 mg sodium, 621 mg potassium. % RDI: 3% calcium, 26% iron, 19% vit A, 12% vit C, 6% folate.

Greek Beef Pitas With Easy Tzatziki

MAKES 4 SERVINGS
HANDS-ON TIME 20 MINUTES
TOTAL TIME 20 MINUTES

EASY TZATZIKI

quarter	English cucumber, seeded
1 cup	2% Greek yogurt or sour cream
2¼ tsp	garlic powder
1 tbsp	lemon juice

PITAS

1 tsp	olive oil
450 g	lean ground beef
half	red onion, chopped
2 tsp	garlic powder
2 tsp	dried oregano
2 tsp	grated lemon zest
½ tsp	each salt and pepper
½ cup	chopped fresh parsley or fresh mint
3 tbsp	lemon juice
4	Greek-style pitas, lightly toasted
16	cherry tomatoes, halved
2 cups	packed baby spinach or baby kale

EASY TZATZIKI Grate cucumber; wrap in clean tea towel and then squeeze to remove excess liquid. In small bowl, stir together cucumber, yogurt, garlic powder and lemon juice. Set aside.

PITAS In large nonstick skillet, heat oil over medium-high heat; cook beef, red onion, garlic powder, oregano, lemon zest, salt and pepper, breaking up with spoon, until beef is no longer pink, 5 to 6 minutes. Remove from heat; stir in parsley and lemon juice. Spread each pita with Easy Tzatziki; top each with beef mixture, tomatoes and spinach. Season with salt to taste. Serve warm.

NUTRITIONAL INFORMATION PER SERVING about 626 cal, 40 g pro, 20 g total fat (7 g sat. fat), 72 g carb (5 g dietary fibre, 7 g sugar), 71 mg chol, 999 mg sodium, 844 mg potassium. % RDI: 30% calcium, 46% iron, 22% vit A, 27% vit C, 54% folate.

VARIATION

Lamb & Olive Pitas

Substitute ground beef with ground lamb. Add 1 green chile, thinly sliced, and ¼ cup chopped pitted black or green olives to skillet along with lamb.

MAKES 8 TO 10 SERVINGS
HANDS-ON TIME 25 MINUTES
TOTAL TIME 3 HOURS

Porchetta-Style Oven Pork Roast

¼ cup	chopped fresh parsley
1 tbsp	each chopped fresh rosemary and fresh sage
3	cloves garlic, pressed or grated
2 tsp	Dijon mustard
1 tsp	fennel seeds, crushed
1 tsp	grated lemon zest
½ tsp	pepper
pinch	each salt and crushed hot pepper flakes
1 tbsp	olive oil
1	boneless pork loin roast (about 1.125 kg)
4	slices prosciutto (about 55 g total)

In bowl, combine parsley, rosemary, sage, garlic, mustard, fennel seeds, lemon zest, pepper, salt and hot pepper flakes; stir in oil. Spread over roast. Cover and refrigerate for 1 hour. *(Make-ahead: Refrigerate for up to 24 hours.)*

Overlapping slices, arrange prosciutto over top of roast. Using kitchen string, tie roast in 5 or 6 places to secure.

Place pork on rack in roasting pan; pour in ½ cup water. Roast in 350°F oven until instant-read thermometer inserted in thickest part reads 155°F, 1½ to 1¾ hours.

Transfer to cutting board and tent with foil; let stand for 10 minutes before carving into ½-inch thick slices.

NUTRITIONAL INFORMATION PER EACH OF 10 SERVINGS about 201 cal, 27 g pro, 9 g total fat (3 g sat. fat), 1 g carb (trace dietary fibre, 0 g sugar), 66 mg chol, 191 mg sodium, 372 mg potassium. % RDI: 1% calcium, 6% iron, 2% vit A, 5% vit C, 2% folate.

VARIATION

Porchetta-Style Barbecue Pork Roast

Follow first 2 paragraphs as directed. Set foil drip pan over 1 burner of 2-burner barbecue or centre burner of 3-burner barbecue. Heat remaining burner(s) to medium.

Place pork on greased grill over drip pan; close lid and grill until instant-read thermometer inserted into thickest part reads 155°F, about 1½ hours.

Transfer to cutting board and tent with foil; let stand for 10 minutes before carving into ½-inch thick slices.

Souvlaki-Style Pork Tenderloin
With Mixed Vegetables

MAKES 4 SERVINGS
HANDS-ON TIME 25 MINUTES
TOTAL TIME 30 MINUTES

PORK TENDERLOIN

450 g	pork tenderloin
2 tsp	dried oregano
½ tsp	pepper
¼ tsp	salt
2 tsp	olive oil
450 g	sweet potatoes, peeled and cut in ½-inch chunks
1	red onion, cut in ¾-inch chunks
2	cloves garlic, minced
½ cup	sodium-reduced chicken broth
2	zucchini, cut in ¾-inch chunks
1	sweet red pepper, cut in ¾-inch chunks
4 tsp	lemon juice

GARLIC YOGURT SAUCE

⅓ cup	0% Greek yogurt
1	small clove garlic, minced

PORK TENDERLOIN Sprinkle pork with ½ tsp of the oregano and half each of the pepper and salt.

In large nonstick skillet, heat half of the oil over medium-high heat; brown pork all over, about 5 minutes. Transfer to foil-lined rimmed baking sheet; bake in 425°F oven until instant-read thermometer inserted into thickest part reads 155°F or juices run clear when pork is pierced and just a hint of pink remains inside, about 12 minutes. Transfer to cutting board; let stand for 3 minutes before slicing.

Meanwhile, in same pan, heat remaining oil over medium heat; cook sweet potatoes, stirring, until lightly browned, about 3 minutes. Stir in red onion, garlic and remaining oregano. Cook, stirring often, until onions are slightly softened, about 2 minutes.

Add broth and ¼ cup water; bring to boil. Reduce heat, cover and simmer just until sweet potatoes are tender, about 6 minutes. Add zucchini, red pepper and remaining pepper and salt; cook, stirring, until zucchini is tender, about 3 minutes. Stir in lemon juice. Transfer to platter; add pork.

GARLIC YOGURT SAUCE Stir together yogurt and garlic; serve with pork and vegetables.

NUTRITIONAL INFORMATION PER SERVING about 293 cal, 31 g pro, 5 g total fat (1 g sat. fat), 32 g carb (5 g dietary fibre, 13 g sugar), 62 mg chol, 309 mg sodium, 984 mg potassium. % RDI: 10% calcium, 21% iron, 174% vit A, 125% vit C, 24% folate.

TIP FROM THE TEST KITCHEN

Pork tenderloin is a Test Kitchen favourite—it cooks quickly, and one tenderloin is about the right size for four servings.

MAKES 4 SERVINGS
HANDS-ON TIME 15 MINUTES
TOTAL TIME 25 MINUTES

Pork Chops Niçoise

4	bone-in pork chops (about 750 g total)
½ tsp	salt
½ tsp	pepper
2 tsp	canola oil
1	onion, chopped
4	garlic cloves, minced
1 tsp	herbes de Provence or dried basil
4	plum tomatoes, chopped
half	green pepper, chopped
½ cup	black olives, pitted
2 tbsp	chopped fresh parsley

Trim fat from chops; sprinkle with salt and pepper. In skillet, heat oil over medium-high heat; cook chops, turning halfway through, until browned, 3 to 5 minutes. Transfer to plate; keep warm.

Drain all but 1 tbsp fat from pan. Add onion, garlic and herbes de Provence; cook over medium heat, stirring occasionally, until onions are softened, about 5 minutes. Add tomatoes and green pepper; reduce heat and simmer, uncovered, for 10 minutes.

Return chops and any accumulated juices to pan, turning to coat with sauce. Add olives; simmer until juices run clear when pork is pierced and just a hint of pink remains inside, about 5 minutes. Serve sprinkled with parsley.

NUTRITIONAL INFORMATION PER SERVING about 246 cal, 25 g pro, 13 g total fat (3 g sat. fat), 9 g carb, 67 mg chol, 497 mg sodium. % RDI: 5% calcium, 16% iron, 10% vit A, 47% vit C, 8% folate.

SERVE WITH

Garlicky Chickpea Mash

In saucepan, heat 1 tbsp olive oil over medium-high heat; add 6 garlic cloves, minced. Cook, stirring, until fragrant, about 1 minute. Stir in 1 can (540 mL) chickpeas, drained and rinsed; ⅓ cup water; and pinch pepper. Cook until warmed through, about 2 minutes. Using potato masher, coarsely mash.

North African Pork Chops
With Cauliflower Couscous

MAKES 4 SERVINGS
HANDS-ON TIME 15 MINUTES
TOTAL TIME 15 MINUTES

1	small head cauliflower, cut in florets (about 7 cups)
2½ tsp	olive oil
½ tsp	each salt and pepper
½ cup	chopped fresh cilantro
1 tsp	ras el hanout
4	boneless pork loin chops (about 450 g total)
1	can (796 mL) diced tomatoes
3 tbsp	tomato paste
½ tsp	onion powder
¼ tsp	garlic powder

In food processor, pulse cauliflower into rice-size pieces. Spread onto parchment paper–lined rimmed baking sheet; drizzle with ½ tsp of the oil and sprinkle with half each of the salt and pepper. Toss to coat. Roast in 400°F oven, stirring once, until dry, about 10 minutes. Stir in half of the cilantro.

Meanwhile, sprinkle pork with remaining salt and pepper; rub all over with half of the ras el hanout. In large nonstick skillet, heat remaining oil over medium-high heat; cook pork, turning once, until juices run clear when pork is pierced and just a hint of pink remains inside, 6 to 8 minutes. Transfer to plate; keep warm.

In same pan, bring tomatoes, tomato paste, onion powder, garlic powder and remaining ras el hanout to boil over medium-high heat; cook, stirring, until thickened, about 4 minutes. Stir in remaining cilantro. Add chops and any accumulated juices; cook until heated through. Serve over cauliflower mixture.

NUTRITIONAL INFORMATION PER SERVING about 324 cal, 31 g pro, 14 g total fat (5 g sat. fat), 20 g carb (9 g dietary fibre, 10 g sugar), 61 mg chol, 711 mg sodium, 1,233 mg potassium. % RDI: 12% calcium, 29% iron, 9% vit A, 210% vit C, 52% folate.

TIP FROM THE TEST KITCHEN

Ras el hanout is a North African spice blend, available in Middle Eastern grocery stores and specialty spice shops. To make your own, mix together ½ tsp each ground cumin, ground ginger, turmeric and salt; ¼ tsp each granulated sugar and pepper; and pinch each cayenne pepper, cinnamon, ground allspice, ground fennel seeds and ground cloves.

MAKES 4 SERVINGS
HANDS-ON TIME 15 MINUTES
TOTAL TIME 20 MINUTES

Quick Chorizo & Mixed Bean Stew

1 tsp	olive oil
450 g	fresh chorizo sausage, casings removed
1	onion, thinly sliced
4	cloves garlic, minced
1 tsp	dried thyme
¼ tsp	smoked paprika
¼ tsp	pepper
1	can (540 mL) no-salt-added white kidney beans, drained and rinsed
1	can (540 mL) no-salt-added mixed beans, drained and rinsed
1 cup	sodium-reduced chicken broth
2 cups	packed baby spinach

In large deep skillet, heat oil over medium-high heat; cook chorizo and onion, breaking up chorizo with wooden spoon, until onion begins to soften, about 5 minutes.

Add garlic, thyme, paprika and pepper; cook, stirring, for 1 minute.

Stir in kidney beans, mixed beans, broth and 1 cup water; bring to boil. Reduce heat and simmer until slightly thickened, 8 to 10 minutes. Stir in spinach; cook just until wilted, about 2 minutes.

NUTRITIONAL INFORMATION PER SERVING about 495 cal, 35 g pro, 17 g total fat (5 g sat. fat), 52 g carb (18 g dietary fibre, 3 g sugar), 64 mg chol, 935 mg sodium, 937 mg potassium. % RDI: 24% calcium, 41% iron, 16% vit A, 7% vit C, 32% folate.

TIP FROM THE TEST KITCHEN

In the Test Kitchen, we often use no-salt-added beans; they allow more control over the salt content and flavour of a dish.

Honey Balsamic Pork Chops
With Roasted Peppers

MAKES 4 SERVINGS
HANDS-ON TIME 20 MINUTES
TOTAL TIME 30 MINUTES

2	sweet red peppers, cut in 2-inch pieces
1	red onion, cut in 2-inch pieces
4 tsp	olive oil
1½ tsp	Italian herb seasoning
½ tsp	each salt and pepper
⅓ cup	cubed feta cheese (about 50 g)
2 tbsp	liquid honey
1 tbsp	balsamic vinegar
2	cloves garlic, pressed or finely grated
2 tsp	Dijon mustard
4	bone-in centre-cut pork loin chops (about 850 g total)
2 tbsp	chopped fresh parsley

In large bowl, toss together red peppers, red onion, half of the oil, the Italian seasoning and half each of the salt and pepper. Arrange in single layer on generously greased rimmed baking sheet. Sprinkle with feta. Roast in 425°F oven, turning once, until tender and golden, about 20 minutes.

Meanwhile, in small bowl, stir together honey, vinegar, garlic and mustard. Sprinkle pork with remaining salt and pepper. In large nonstick skillet, heat remaining oil over medium heat; cook pork, turning once, until just a hint of pink remains inside, 8 to 10 minutes. Pour honey mixture over pork chops; cook, turning to coat, until glazed, about 1 minute.

Divide pork and vegetables among 4 serving plates; sprinkle with parsley.

NUTRITIONAL INFORMATION PER SERVING about 436 cal, 37 g pro, 22 g total fat (8 g sat. fat), 22 g carb (2 g dietary fibre, 16 g sugar), 124 mg chol, 554 mg sodium, 810 mg potassium. % RDI: 12% calcium, 15% iron, 26% vit A, 225% vit C, 13% folate.

MAKES 4 SERVINGS
HANDS-ON TIME 15 MINUTES
TOTAL TIME 15 MINUTES

Sticky Lamb Chops
With Parmesan Cauliflower

LAMB

2 tbsp	liquid honey
2	cloves garlic, pressed or finely grated
2 tsp	lime juice
1 tsp	Dijon mustard
8	frenched lamb chops (about 565 g total)
¼ tsp	each salt and pepper

PARMESAN CAULIFLOWER

1	small cauliflower, cut in bite-size florets
¼ cup	finely grated Parmesan cheese
¼ cup	chopped fresh parsley
2 tbsp	finely chopped pitted Niçoise olives
2 tbsp	extra-virgin olive oil
1 tbsp	lime juice
pinch	each salt and pepper

LAMB In small bowl, whisk together honey, garlic, lime juice and mustard. Set aside.

Sprinkle lamb with salt and pepper. Place on greased grill over medium-high heat; close lid and grill, turning once, until desired doneness, about 5 minutes for medium-rare. Brush all over with honey mixture; cook until glazed and sticky, 1 to 2 minutes.

PARMESAN CAULIFLOWER While lamb is cooking, in steamer basket set over saucepan of boiling water, steam cauliflower, covered, until tender-crisp, about 5 minutes.

In large bowl, stir together Parmesan, parsley, olives, oil, lime juice, salt and pepper. Stir in cauliflower. Serve with lamb.

NUTRITIONAL INFORMATION PER SERVING about 378 cal, 24 g pro, 25 g total fat (9 g sat. fat), 16 g carb (4 g dietary fibre, 11 g sugar), 54 mg chol, 376 mg sodium, 456 mg potassium. % RDI: 11% calcium, 15% iron, 4% vit A, 108% vit C, 35% folate.

TIP FROM THE TEST KITCHEN

You can substitute the lamb chops with four bone-in pork rib chops (about 790 g total), grilled for four minutes per side.

Grilled Lamb Chops
With Fennel & Mint-Almond Pesto

MAKES 4 SERVINGS
HANDS-ON TIME 15 MINUTES
TOTAL TIME 15 MINUTES

GRILLED FENNEL & LAMB Place fennel and red onion on greased grill over medium-high heat; close lid and grill, turning once, until softened and charred, about 10 minutes. Transfer to bowl; toss with 1 tsp of the oil, the vinegar and half each of the salt and pepper.

While vegetables are grilling, rub lamb all over with remaining oil, salt, pepper and the oregano. Place on greased grill over medium-high heat; close lid and grill, turning once, until desired doneness, about 8 minutes for medium-rare.

MINT-ALMOND PESTO In food processor, pulse almonds with garlic until coarsely ground. Add mint, parsley, Parmesan, salt and pepper; pulse 6 times. With motor running, add oil in thin steady stream, blending until smooth. Scrape into small bowl; stir in lemon juice.

ASSEMBLY Top lamb chops with pesto and serve with vegetables.

NUTRITIONAL INFORMATION PER SERVING about 404 cal, 26 g pro, 28 g total fat (10 g sat. fat), 12 g carb (4 g dietary fibre, 6 g sugar), 61 mg chol, 479 mg sodium, 758 mg potassium. % RDI: 10% calcium, 22% iron, 6% vit A, 23% vit C, 21% folate.

GRILLED FENNEL & LAMB

- **1** bulb fennel, trimmed, cored and sliced in ⅓-inch thick pieces
- **1** small red onion, cut in 8 wedges
- **1 tbsp** olive oil
- **1 tbsp** balsamic vinegar
- **½ tsp** salt
- **¼ tsp** pepper
- **8** frenched lamb chops (about 600 g total)
- **1 tsp** dried oregano

MINT-ALMOND PESTO

- **¼ cup** blanched almonds, toasted
- **1** clove garlic, halved
- **½ cup** fresh mint leaves
- **½ cup** fresh parsley leaves
- **2 tbsp** finely grated Parmesan cheese
- **¼ tsp** salt
- **pinch** pepper
- **¼ cup** extra-virgin olive oil
- **1 tsp** lemon juice

MAKES 4 SERVINGS
HANDS-ON TIME 25 MINUTES
TOTAL TIME 40 MINUTES

Herbed Lamb Chops
With Zucchini-Tomato Gratin

1 cup	bottled strained tomatoes (passata)
1 tbsp	pesto
2	medium zucchini, cut in ⅛-inch slices
1	plum tomato, cut in ⅛-inch slices
2 tbsp	olive oil
¾ tsp	herbes de Provence or dried Italian herb seasoning
¼ tsp	each salt and pepper
⅓ cup	crumbled feta cheese
1 tbsp	coarsely chopped fresh mint
8	lamb loin chops (about 675 g total), trimmed

Mix passata with pesto; spread in 8-cup oval baking dish.

Arrange zucchini and tomato in single layer over large clean tea towel; top with second towel and gently press to absorb excess moisture.

In bowl, toss together zucchini, 1 tbsp of the oil, ½ tsp of the herbes de Provence and half each of the salt and pepper.

Arrange zucchini and tomato in overlapping concentric circles on passata mixture, adding tomato slice after every few zucchini slices. Bake in 425°F oven until tender, 18 to 20 minutes. Sprinkle with feta; broil until feta is slightly golden, 2 to 3 minutes. Sprinkle with mint.

Meanwhile, season lamb with remaining herbes de Provence, salt and pepper. In large skillet, heat remaining oil over medium-high heat; cook lamb until browned and centre is medium-rare to medium, 3 to 5 minutes per side. Serve with gratin.

NUTRITIONAL INFORMATION PER SERVING about 272 cal, 23 g pro, 17 g total fat (6 g sat. fat), 8 g carb (2 g dietary fibre, 5 g sugar), 58 mg chol, 512 mg sodium, 608 mg potassium. % RDI: 9% calcium, 21% iron, 13% vit A, 12% vit C, 15% folate.

Roast Lamb With Tapenade

MAKES 8 TO 10 SERVINGS
HANDS-ON TIME 15 MINUTES
TOTAL TIME 2 HOURS

TAPENADE

1	clove garlic, minced
1 cup	drained oil-cured black olives, pitted
2	anchovy fillets (or 2 tsp anchovy paste)
1 tbsp	rinsed drained capers
¼ tsp	pepper
2 tbsp	extra-virgin olive oil

ROAST LAMB

1	boneless leg of lamb (about 1.75 kg)
1 tbsp	extra-virgin olive oil
¼ tsp	each salt and pepper

TAPENADE In food processor, coarsely chop together garlic, olives, anchovies, capers and pepper; pulse in oil and ¼ cup water until in chunky paste. Set aside.

ROAST LAMB Open leg of lamb and place on work surface, fat side down. Spread with tapenade; roll up and tie with kitchen string at 1½-inch intervals.

Place lamb on rack in roasting pan. Rub all over with oil; sprinkle with salt and pepper. Roast in 325°F oven until instant-read thermometer inserted in centre reads 145°F for medium-rare, about 1½ hours, or 160°F for medium. Transfer to cutting board and tent with foil; let stand for 15 minutes before carving.

Meanwhile, skim fat from pan juices; strain juices into gravy boat. Serve with lamb.

NUTRITIONAL INFORMATION PER EACH OF 10 SERVINGS about 291 cal, 29 g pro, 18 g total fat (4 g sat. fat), 1 g carb (1 g dietary fibre), 91 mg chol, 644 mg sodium. % RDI: 2% calcium, 21% iron, 8% folate.

SERVE WITH

Green Beans With Pine Nuts

In large saucepan of boiling salted water, cook 1 kg green beans, trimmed, until tender-crisp, about 7 minutes. Drain in colander. In same pan, heat 1 tsp extra-virgin olive oil over medium heat; cook ¼ cup pine nuts, stirring frequently, until golden, about 3 minutes. Add 2 tsp grated lemon rind; cook for 1 minute. Mix in 1 tbsp lemon juice and 2 tsp extra-virgin olive oil. Return beans to pan; toss to coat and heat through.

MAKES 8 TO 10 SERVINGS
HANDS-ON TIME 30 MINUTES
TOTAL TIME 3¼ HOURS

Stuffed Leg of Lamb
With Artichokes, Spinach & Red Peppers

2	sweet red peppers, halved and cored
1	pkg (454 g) baby spinach
1	can (400 mL) water-packed artichoke hearts, drained and coarsely chopped
1 cup	fresh bread crumbs
1 tbsp	lemon juice
½ tsp	salt
2.7 kg	butterflied boneless leg of lamb
½ tsp	pepper
2 tbsp	Dijon mustard
1 tbsp	grated lemon zest
1 tbsp	liquid honey

Place red pepper halves, cut side down, on foil-lined baking sheet; broil, turning occasionally, until softened and charred, 12 to 15 minutes. Let cool. Peel off blackened skin and discard; slice peppers lengthwise into strips.

Meanwhile, in large saucepan of boiling water, blanch spinach just until wilted, about 1 minute; drain and rinse under cold water. One handful at a time, squeeze excess water out of spinach. In bowl, combine spinach, red peppers, artichoke hearts, bread crumbs, lemon juice and a generous pinch of the salt. *(Make-ahead: Let cool. Refrigerate in airtight container for up to 24 hours.)*

Unroll lamb on work surface, skin side down; trim off any excess fat or sinew. Leaving 1-inch border at edges, spread filling evenly over lamb; starting at one long side, roll up. Using kitchen string, tie tightly at 2-inch intervals. Rub lamb all over with pepper and remaining salt.

Whisk together mustard, lemon zest and honey; brush all over lamb.

Place lamb on greased rack in roasting pan; pour 1 cup water into pan. Bake in 375°F oven, tenting with foil if browning too quickly, until instant-read thermometer inserted in centre reads 145°F for medium-rare, 2½ to 3 hours.

Transfer to cutting board; tent with foil. Let stand for 15 minutes before carving.

NUTRITIONAL INFORMATION PER EACH OF 10 SERVINGS about 427 cal, 59 g pro, 17 g total fat (7 g sat. fat), 10 g carb (3 g dietary fibre, 3 g sugar), 133 mg chol, 440 mg sodium, 1,034 mg potassium. % RDI: 12% calcium, 39% iron, 53% vit A, 75% vit C, 53% folate.

Spiced Lamb Platter
With Hummus & Quick-Pickled Onions

MAKES 4 SERVINGS
HANDS-ON TIME 25 MINUTES
TOTAL TIME 30 MINUTES

¾ cup	cider vinegar
2 tsp	granulated sugar
¼ tsp	salt
half	red onion, very thinly sliced
1 tbsp	olive oil
450 g	ground lamb
1	yellow onion, finely chopped
3	cloves garlic, minced
1 tsp	chili powder
1 tsp	ground coriander
½ tsp	ground cumin
pinch	each pepper, cinnamon and cayenne pepper
⅓ cup	chopped fresh cilantro
2	small (6 inch) whole wheat pitas, each cut in 8 wedges
¾ cup	hummus

In bowl, whisk together vinegar, sugar and half of the salt; stir in red onion. Let stand for 25 minutes, stirring occasionally. *(Make-ahead: Refrigerate for up to 24 hours.)* Drain.

Meanwhile, in nonstick skillet, heat half of the oil over medium-high heat; cook lamb, breaking up with spoon, until browned and crisp, about 5 minutes. Drain, discarding fat; transfer lamb to bowl.

In same skillet, heat remaining oil over medium heat. Add yellow onion; cook, stirring, until golden, about 5 minutes. Stir in garlic, chili powder, coriander, cumin, pepper, cinnamon, cayenne pepper and remaining salt; cook for 1 minute. Stir in lamb; cook until warmed, about 5 minutes. Stir in cilantro.

Meanwhile, arrange pitas in single layer on baking sheet. Bake in 400°F oven until crisp and golden, 6 to 8 minutes. *(Make-ahead: Store in airtight container for up to 24 hours.)*

Spread lamb mixture on platter; top with hummus and pickled onions. Serve with pitas.

NUTRITIONAL INFORMATION PER SERVING about 394 cal, 25 g pro, 20 g total fat (6 g sat. fat), 31 g carb (6 g dietary fibre, 5 g sugar), 66 mg chol, 490 mg sodium, 579 mg potassium. % RDI: 5% calcium, 26% iron, 3% vit A, 7% vit C, 36% folate.

MAKES 4 SERVINGS
HANDS-ON TIME 20 MINUTES
TOTAL TIME 30 MINUTES

Lamb & Za'atar Flatbread
With Pea Shoots

FLATBREAD

1 tbsp	olive oil
250 g	ground lamb
2 tbsp	za'atar
1 tsp	ground cumin
¼ tsp	each salt and pepper
375 g	prepared pizza dough
1 cup	extra-smooth ricotta cheese
1 tsp	grated lemon zest
2 tbsp	lemon juice
1	corn cob, husked
¼ tsp	hot pepper flakes

TOPPING

2 cups	pea shoots, halved
1 tsp	lemon juice
1 tsp	olive oil
pinch	salt

FLATBREAD In nonstick skillet, heat ½ tsp of the oil over medium-high heat; cook lamb, breaking up with spoon, until browned, about 4 minutes. Stir in 4 tsp of the za'atar, the cumin, salt and pepper. Using slotted spoon, transfer to bowl. Set aside.

On lightly floured work surface, roll out or press dough into 16- x 8-inch oval. Transfer to greased large rimless baking sheet.

In small bowl, stir together ricotta, lemon zest and lemon juice. In separate small bowl, mix remaining oil with remaining za'atar; brush over top of dough. Dot with ricotta mixture, spreading slightly. Sprinkle with lamb. Bake on bottom rack of 500°F oven until beginning to brown, about 8 minutes.

Cut kernels from corn cob; sprinkle over flatbread. Bake on bottom rack of 500°F oven until bottom is crisp and golden, about 10 minutes. Sprinkle with hot pepper flakes.

TOPPING Stir together pea shoots, lemon juice, oil and salt; sprinkle over flatbread.

NUTRITIONAL INFORMATION PER SERVING about 537 cal, 28 g pro, 21 g total fat (9 g sat. fat), 57 g carb (4 g dietary fibre, 5 g sugar), 56 mg chol, 684 mg sodium, 307 mg potassium. % RDI: 14% calcium, 36% iron, 21% vit A, 20% vit C, 14% folate.

TIP FROM THE TEST KITCHEN

Check your local farmers' market or Asian grocery stores for fresh pea shoots—they're the curly, leafy tendrils of the pea plant.

Dukkah Chicken Skewers
With Grilled Zucchini Ribbons

MAKES 4 SERVINGS
HANDS-ON TIME 15 MINUTES
TOTAL TIME 30 MINUTES

2 tbsp	vegetable oil
1 tbsp	liquid honey
1 tbsp	tahini
1 tbsp	lemon juice
½ tsp	salt (optional)
½ tsp	pepper
450 g	boneless skinless chicken thighs, cut in 1-inch pieces
½ cup	Dukkah Spice Blend (see recipe, below)
1	small zucchini, cut in long thin ribbons
1	small red onion, cut in 1-inch pieces

In large bowl, whisk together oil, honey, tahini, lemon juice, salt (if using) and pepper. Add chicken, turning to coat. *(Make-ahead: Cover and refrigerate for up to 24 hours.)*

Place dukkah in shallow dish; spoon 1 tbsp into bowl and set aside. Remove chicken from marinade, letting excess drip off. Discard marinade. Dredge chicken in dukkah, pressing to adhere. Alternately thread chicken, zucchini and red onion onto 6 metal or soaked wooden skewers. *(Make-ahead: Cover and refrigerate for up to 24 hours.)*

Place skewers on greased grill over medium heat; close lid and grill, turning once, until chicken is browned and no longer pink inside, about 15 minutes. Transfer to serving platter; sprinkle reserved dukkah over top.

NUTRITIONAL INFORMATION PER SERVING about 318 cal, 25 g pro, 20 g total fat (3 g sat. fat), 12 g carb (3 g dietary fibre, 6 g sugar), 93 mg chol, 260 mg sodium, 523 mg potassium. % RDI: 7% calcium, 24% iron, 6% vit A, 15% vit C, 15% folate.

Dukkah Spice Blend

In food processor, pulse together 1 cup skinned toasted hazelnuts, ½ cup toasted sesame seeds, 6 tbsp coriander seeds, 2 tbsp cumin seeds, 4 tsp peppercorns and 2 tsp salt until finely chopped. Store in airtight container in refrigerator for up to 1 month.

MAKES 8 SERVINGS
HANDS-ON TIME 25 MINUTES
TOTAL TIME 1¼ HOURS

Garlicky Cornish Hens
With Lemon & Herbs

1 tsp	grated lemon zest
¼ cup	lemon juice
2 tbsp	olive oil
4	cloves garlic, pressed or finely grated
1 tbsp	each chopped fresh thyme and fresh oregano
2 tsp	liquid honey
1 tsp	salt
½ tsp	pepper
4	Cornish hens (each about 580 g)
1	lemon, halved crosswise

In large bowl, whisk together lemon zest, lemon juice, oil, garlic, thyme, oregano, honey, salt and pepper. Set aside. *(Make-ahead: Cover and refrigerate for up to 24 hours; whisk before using.)*

Using kitchen shears, cut 1 hen down each side of backbone; discard backbone or reserve for another use. Cut hen in half lengthwise through breastbone. Repeat with remaining hens. *(Make-ahead: Cover and refrigerate for up to 24 hours.)*

Add hens to lemon mixture; toss to coat. Arrange, skin side up, on lightly greased large heavy-duty rimmed baking sheet. Add lemon, cut side up. Bake in 425°F oven, basting twice, until instant-read thermometer inserted in thickest part of thigh reads 185°F, about 45 minutes. Remove hens to platter. Let stand for 5 minutes.

Meanwhile, return lemon to oven; broil, cut side up, until lightly charred, about 1 minute. Serve with hens.

NUTRITIONAL INFORMATION PER SERVING about 333 cal, 25 g pro, 24 g total fat (6 g sat. fat), 3 g carb (trace dietary fibre, 2 g sugar), 146 mg chol, 359 mg sodium, 304 mg potassium. % RDI: 2% calcium, 9% iron, 4% vit A, 13% vit C, 2% folate.

TIP FROM THE TEST KITCHEN

Use a heavy-duty rimmed baking sheet, instead of a roasting pan, to allow for better air circulation around the hens; this helps them brown more evenly.

Chicken Ratatouille
With Lemony Basil Polenta

MAKES 4 SERVINGS
HANDS-ON TIME 30 MINUTES
TOTAL TIME 30 MINUTES

CHICKEN RATATOUILLE Sprinkle chicken with half of the oregano. In Dutch oven or large heavy-bottomed saucepan, heat 1 tsp of the oil over medium heat; cook chicken until golden, about 5 minutes. Using slotted spoon, transfer to plate.

Add remaining oil to pan; cook eggplant and onion, stirring frequently, until beginning to soften, about 5 minutes. Stir in zucchini, red pepper and garlic; cook, stirring occasionally, until tender-crisp, about 4 minutes.

Stir in tomatoes, pepper, hot pepper flakes, salt and remaining oregano. Return chicken to pan; cook, stirring occasionally, until vegetables are tender and juices run clear when thickest part of chicken is pierced, about 10 minutes.

LEMONY BASIL POLENTA Meanwhile, in saucepan, heat oil over medium heat; cook onion and garlic, stirring occasionally, until softened, about 5 minutes.

Add broth, ⅓ cup water, the pepper and salt; bring to boil. Reduce heat to medium-low. Gradually whisk in cornmeal; cook, stirring often, until polenta is thick enough to mound on spoon, 5 to 10 minutes. Stir in lemon zest, lemon juice and butter. Fold in basil. Serve topped with ratatouille.

NUTRITIONAL INFORMATION PER SERVING about 405 cal, 27 g pro, 17 g total fat (5 g sat. fat), 36 g carb (5 g dietary fibre, 8 g sugar), 102 mg chol, 264 mg sodium, 819 mg potassium. % RDI: 7% calcium, 24% iron, 21% vit A, 122% vit C, 31% folate.

CHICKEN RATATOUILLE

450 g	boneless skinless chicken thighs, quartered
1 tsp	dried oregano
2 tbsp	olive oil
1	Asian eggplant, thinly sliced
half	onion, thinly sliced
1	zucchini, thinly sliced
1	sweet red pepper, chopped
3	cloves garlic, minced
1	can (400 mL) diced tomatoes
½ tsp	pepper
¼ tsp	hot pepper flakes
pinch	salt

LEMONY BASIL POLENTA

1 tsp	olive oil
half	onion, diced
3	cloves garlic, minced
2 cups	no-salt-added chicken broth
¼ tsp	pepper
pinch	salt
¾ cup	cornmeal
1 tsp	grated lemon zest
1 tbsp	lemon juice
1 tbsp	unsalted butter
¼ cup	torn basil leaves

MAKES 8 SERVINGS
HANDS-ON TIME 20 MINUTES
TOTAL TIME 1¼ HOURS

Chicken Zarzuela

16	skinless chicken thighs (about 2 kg total)
1 tsp	salt
½ tsp	pepper
2 tbsp	olive oil
½ cup	dry white wine (or chicken broth plus 2 tbsp white wine vinegar)
2	Spanish onions, chopped
6	cloves garlic, minced
1	can (796 mL) whole tomatoes
4 tsp	sweet paprika
1 tsp	dried marjoram (or dried oregano)
¼ tsp	saffron threads
⅓ cup	ground almonds
1 tbsp	lemon juice
1 cup	large green olives, pitted and halved
¼ cup	chopped fresh parsley

Sprinkle chicken with half of the salt and the pepper. In large nonstick skillet, heat 1 tbsp of the oil over medium-high heat; working in batches, cook chicken, turning occasionally until lightly browned all over, 4 to 6 minutes. Transfer to 13- x 9-inch glass baking dish.

Drain fat from skillet. Add wine; bring to boil, stirring to scrape up brown bits. Pour over chicken.

Wipe out skillet; heat remaining oil over medium heat. Cook onions and ⅔ of the garlic, stirring often, until golden, about 4 minutes. Add tomatoes, paprika, marjoram and remaining salt, breaking up tomatoes with wooden spoon. Bring to boil; pour over chicken.

Cover loosely with foil and bake in 375°F oven until juices run clear when thickest part of chicken is pierced, about 40 minutes.

Meanwhile, crumble saffron into bowl; pour in 2 tbsp water and let sit for 5 minutes. Add almonds, remaining garlic and the lemon juice. Uncover casserole; stir in almond mixture and olives.

Bake until heated through, about 10 minutes. *(Make-ahead: Let cool for 30 minutes. Transfer to airtight container. Refrigerate, uncovered, until cold. Cover and refrigerate for up to 1 day. Or freeze for up to 2 weeks; thaw in refrigerator for 24 hours. Reheat in 375°F oven, about 40 minutes.)* Stir in parsley.

NUTRITIONAL INFORMATION PER SERVING about 356 cal, 35 g pro, 17 g total fat (3 g sat. fat), 16 g carb, 138 mg chol, 1,040 mg sodium. % RDI: 9% calcium, 26% iron, 17% vit A, 35% vit C, 15% folate.

Speedy Asparagus & Chicken Piccata With Herbed Couscous

MAKES 4 SERVINGS
HANDS-ON TIME 15 MINUTES
TOTAL TIME 15 MINUTES

PICCATA

450 g	boneless skinless chicken breast cutlets
¼ tsp	each salt and pepper
2 tbsp	all-purpose flour
1 tbsp	olive oil
1	bunch (about 450 g) asparagus, trimmed and cut in 2-inch lengths
1 tbsp	butter
½ cup	dry white wine
1 cup	sodium-reduced chicken broth
1 tbsp	capers, drained and rinsed
1 tbsp	lemon juice

HERBED COUSCOUS

¼ cup	couscous
pinch	each salt and pepper
1 cup	boiling water
¼ cup	chopped fresh parsley
2 tsp	lemon juice

PICCATA Sprinkle chicken with pinch each of the salt and pepper. Sprinkle with 1 tbsp of the flour, turning to coat both sides and shaking off excess. In nonstick skillet, heat 2 tsp of the oil over medium-high heat; cook chicken, turning once, until golden, about 4 minutes. Transfer to plate.

In same pan, heat remaining oil over medium heat; cook asparagus, stirring occasionally, until tender-crisp, about 3 minutes. Transfer to plate.

In same pan, melt butter over medium heat. Gradually whisk in remaining flour; cook, stirring, for 1 minute. Pour in wine; bring to boil over medium heat. Cook, stirring, until reduced by half, about 1 minute.

Pour in broth; bring to boil. Add chicken; cook, stirring until chicken is no longer pink inside and sauce is thickened, about 3 minutes. Stir in capers, lemon juice and remaining salt and pepper. Stir in asparagus.

HERBED COUSCOUS While chicken is cooking, in bowl, whisk together couscous, salt and pepper; pour in boiling water. Cover tightly with plastic wrap; let stand until no liquid remains, about 5 minutes. Fluff with fork. Stir in parsley and lemon juice. Serve with piccata.

NUTRITIONAL INFORMATION PER SERVING: about 339 cal, 32 g pro, 8 g total fat (3 g sat. fat), 29 g carb (2 g dietary fibre, 2 g sugar), 74 mg chol, 454 mg sodium, 554 mg potassium. % RDI: 4% calcium, 14% iron, 12% vit A, 17% vit C, 51% folate.

TIP FROM THE TEST KITCHEN

Can't find chicken cutlets? Buy boneless, skinless whole chicken breasts, cut them in half horizontally and pound to flatten into cutlets.

MAKES 2 SERVINGS
HANDS-ON TIME 20 MINUTES
TOTAL TIME 20 MINUTES

Skillet Mediterranean Chicken

1	large boneless skinless chicken breast (about 225 g)
½ tsp	each dried tarragon and dried oregano
¼ tsp	each salt and pepper
1 tbsp	olive oil
85 g	Broccolini
half	sweet yellow pepper, coarsely chopped
2	cloves garlic, minced
2 tbsp	chopped pitted Kalamata olives
¼ cup	dry white wine
¼ cup	crumbled feta cheese
1 tbsp	chopped fresh basil

Place chicken on cutting board. Holding knife blade parallel to board and with opposite hand on top of chicken, slice chicken horizontally all the way through to form 2 cutlets. Sprinkle both sides of each with tarragon, oregano, salt and pepper.

In large nonstick skillet, heat 1 tsp of the oil over medium-high heat; cook chicken, turning once, until lightly browned, about 4 minutes. Transfer to plate.

In same pan, heat remaining oil over medium-high heat; cook Broccolini, yellow pepper, garlic and olives until fragrant, about 2 minutes. Add chicken and wine; cover and simmer until chicken is no longer pink inside and Broccolini is tender-crisp, 4 to 5 minutes. Remove from heat; sprinkle with feta and basil.

NUTRITIONAL INFORMATION PER SERVING about 289 cal, 31 g pro, 14 g total fat (5 g sat. fat), 10 g carb (2 g dietary fibre, 3 g sugar), 83 mg chol, 1,009 mg sodium, 646 mg potassium. % RDI: 15% calcium, 14% iron, 12% vit A, 160% vit C, 19% folate.

SERVE WITH

Orzo Salad

In saucepan of boiling salted water, cook ½ cup orzo pasta until tender, about 8 minutes. Drain well and transfer to bowl. Add ¾ cup halved cherry tomatoes, 3 tbsp crumbled feta cheese, 2 tbsp chopped fresh basil, 2 tbsp finely diced red onion, 1 tbsp red wine vinegar, 1½ tsp extra-virgin olive oil and pinch each salt and pepper; toss well.

Lightened-Up Chicken Parmigiana
With Garlicky Zucchini & Broccoli

MAKES 4 SERVINGS
HANDS-ON TIME 30 MINUTES
TOTAL TIME 30 MINUTES

2	boneless skinless chicken breasts (about 450 g total), cut in half horizontally
¼ tsp	each salt and pepper
4 tsp	all-purpose flour
1½ tsp	dried oregano
1	egg white
½ cup	panko bread crumbs
6	cloves garlic
4 tsp	olive oil
¼ tsp	hot pepper flakes
2	zucchini, halved lengthwise and sliced crosswise
2½ cups	broccoli florets, cut in bite-size pieces
2 tsp	lemon juice
1	onion, chopped
1½ cups	bottled strained tomatoes (passata)
1 tsp	red wine vinegar
¼ cup	finely grated Parmesan cheese
6	fresh basil leaves, thinly sliced

Sprinkle both sides of chicken with half each of the salt and pepper. In bowl, mix flour with ½ tsp of the oregano. In separate bowl, whisk egg white until frothy. Add bread crumbs to third bowl. Dredge both sides of chicken in flour mixture, shaking off excess. Dip in egg white, letting excess drip off. Press both sides in bread crumbs.

Arrange in single layer in lightly greased 13- x 9-inch baking dish. Bake in 425°F oven until chicken is no longer pink inside, about 18 minutes.

Meanwhile, thinly slice half of the garlic; mince remaining garlic and set aside. In nonstick skillet, heat half of the oil over medium heat; cook sliced garlic and half of the hot pepper flakes, stirring, until fragrant, about 1 minute. Add zucchini, broccoli and remaining salt and pepper; cook, stirring occasionally, just until tender-crisp, about 7 minutes. Remove from heat; stir in lemon juice. Scrape into bowl; keep warm.

In same skillet, heat remaining oil over medium heat; cook onion, remaining oregano and hot pepper flakes, stirring occasionally, until onion is softened and golden, about 5 minutes. Stir in reserved minced garlic; cook until fragrant, about 30 seconds. Stir in passata, vinegar and 2 tbsp water; cook until heated through, about 3 minutes.

Spoon tomato mixture over chicken. Sprinkle with Parmesan. Bake in 425°F oven until cheese is melted, about 2 minutes. Top with basil. Serve with zucchini mixture.

NUTRITIONAL INFORMATION PER SERVING about 307 cal, 33 g pro, 9 g total fat (2 g sat. fat), 23 g carb (4 g dietary fibre, 10 g sugar), 71 mg chol, 520 mg sodium, 1,042 mg potassium. % RDI: 14% calcium, 26% iron, 28% vit A, 77% vit C, 32% folate.

MAKES 4 SERVINGS
HANDS-ON TIME 25 MINUTES
TOTAL TIME 35 MINUTES

Chicken Milanese
With Celery Root Purée & Watercress Salad

CHICKEN MILANESE

450 g	chicken cutlets
½ tsp	each salt and pepper
¼ cup	all-purpose flour
1	large egg
1 tbsp	grainy mustard
1 cup	panko bread crumbs
2 tbsp	vegetable oil

CELERY ROOT PURÉE

1	celery root (about 675 g), peeled and cut in 1-inch chunks
1	russet potato (about 340 g), peeled and cut in 1-inch chunks
2	cloves garlic, smashed
⅓ cup	shredded Gruyère cheese
¼ cup	10% cream
¼ tsp	salt

WATERCRESS SALAD

1½ tbsp	extra-virgin olive oil
1 tbsp	lemon juice
2 cups	lightly packed watercress or arugula

CHICKEN MILANESE Sprinkle chicken with salt and pepper. Place flour in shallow dish. In separate shallow dish, whisk egg with mustard. Place bread crumbs in third shallow dish. Dip chicken into flour, shaking off excess; dip into egg mixture, letting excess drip back into dish. Press into bread crumbs to coat. Place on waxed paper–lined rimmed baking sheet; refrigerate for 10 minutes. *(Make-ahead: Cover and refrigerate for up to 8 hours.)* In large nonstick skillet, heat vegetable oil over medium heat; cook chicken, turning once, until no longer pink inside, 8 to 10 minutes.

CELERY ROOT PURÉE Meanwhile, in large saucepan of boiling salted water, cook celery root, potato and garlic until tender, 12 to 15 minutes. Drain; return to pan. Dry over low heat, shaking pan often, for 1 minute. Transfer to food processor; add Gruyère, cream and salt. Purée until smooth.

WATERCRESS SALAD In bowl, whisk olive oil with lemon juice; toss with watercress. Serve over chicken and celery root purée.

NUTRITIONAL INFORMATION PER SERVING about 492 cal, 36 g pro, 20 g total fat (5 g sat. fat), 42 g carb (5 g dietary fibre, 16 g sugar), 124 mg chol, 1,459 mg sodium, 1,088 mg potassium. % RDI: 20% calcium, 20% iron, 12% vit A, 47% vit C, 16% folate.

TIP FROM THE TEST KITCHEN

Boiling pasta, potatoes and some other vegetables, including celery root, in salted water brightens their flavours. When we call for "salted water," we use 2 tbsp salt in 5 L water (to cook about 450 g of potatoes or pasta); "lightly salted water" has half as much salt.

Spanish Chicken Stew

MAKES 10 SERVINGS
HANDS-ON TIME 35 MINUTES
TOTAL TIME 50 MINUTES

1 tsp	vegetable oil
900 g	boneless skinless chicken thighs, cut in ¾-inch pieces
2 cups	sliced leeks, white and light green parts only (about 2 small leeks)
6	cloves garlic, thinly sliced
1 tbsp	tomato paste
¼ tsp	salt
1	jar (300 mL) roasted red peppers, drained and chopped
1	can (796 mL) whole tomatoes
675 g	mini yellow-fleshed potatoes, scrubbed and halved
1 cup	frozen peas, thawed
2 tbsp	chopped fresh flatleaf parsley

In Dutch oven or large heavy-bottomed saucepan, heat oil over medium-high heat. Working in batches, brown chicken, about 15 minutes. Remove from pan and set aside.

Add leeks and garlic to pan; cook over medium-high heat until garlic is fragrant, about 1 minute. Return chicken to pan; cook, stirring frequently, until leeks begin to soften, about 4 minutes.

Add tomato paste, salt and red peppers; cook, stirring, for 2 minutes. Stir in whole tomatoes, breaking up with wooden spoon; bring to boil. Reduce heat and simmer for 10 minutes.

Meanwhile, in large saucepan of boiling lightly salted water, cook potatoes just until tender, about 8 minutes. Drain and add to stew. Simmer until stew is thickened, about 15 minutes.

Stir in peas and parsley; cook until peas are warmed through.

NUTRITIONAL INFORMATION PER SERVING about 218 cal, 21 g pro, 5 g total fat (1 g sat. fat), 23 g carb (3 g dietary fibre, 6 g sugar), 75 mg chol, 569 mg sodium, 708 mg potassium. % RDI: 6% calcium, 24% iron, 13% vit A, 95% vit C, 15% folate.

MAKES 4 SERVINGS
HANDS-ON TIME 20 MINUTES
TOTAL TIME 30 MINUTES

Chicken Meatballs
With Peppers & Spinach

450 g	ground chicken
⅓ cup	panko bread crumbs
⅜ cup	jarred basil pesto
½ tsp	salt (optional)
2 tbsp	olive oil
1	sweet yellow pepper, seeded and coarsely chopped
3	cloves garlic, pressed or finely grated
2 tsp	lemon zest
2 tbsp	lemon juice
½ tsp	pepper
2	bunches spinach (about 400 g total), trimmed

In large bowl, mix together chicken, bread crumbs, ¼ cup of the pesto and the salt (if using).

Firmly roll by 1 tbsp into balls. In large skillet, heat oil over medium heat. Add meatballs; cook, stirring occasionally, until browned, about 2 minutes. Add yellow pepper; cook, stirring occasionally, until meatballs are no longer pink inside, 3 to 6 minutes. Transfer meatballs and yellow pepper to separate plates.

In same skillet, add remaining pesto, the garlic, lemon juice and pepper. Add half of the spinach; cover and cook for 1 minute. Stir, add remaining spinach; cover and cook for 1 minute. Uncover, stir and continue cooking until spinach is wilted. Add meatballs and yellow pepper; stir to combine. Stir in lemon zest. Serve with pasta.

NUTRITIONAL INFORMATION PER SERVING about 454 cal, 25 g pro, 32 g total fat (7 g sat. fat), 17 g carb (4 g dietary fibre, 4 g sugar), 88 mg chol, 393 mg sodium, 634 mg potassium. % RDI: 18% calcium, 38% iron, 108% vit A, 185% vit C, 72% folate.

TIP FROM THE TEST KITCHEN

Use leftover meatballs to make cheesy meatball subs. Split and toast soft French rolls. Spoon in the meatball mixture, top with mozzarella or provolone cheese, and broil until cheese is melted and bubbly.

Mediterranean Chicken Pita Burgers

MAKES 4 SERVINGS
HANDS-ON TIME 15 MINUTES
TOTAL TIME 25 MINUTES

BURGERS

¼ cup	shredded English cucumber
½ cup	Greek yogurt
1½ tsp	harissa paste
1½ tsp	liquid honey
½ tsp	lemon juice
450 g	lean ground chicken
2	cloves garlic, minced
1	large egg, lightly beaten
2 tbsp	finely chopped fresh mint
1 tbsp	ground coriander
2 tsp	ground cumin
1 tsp	salt
4	pita pockets

TOPPINGS (OPTIONAL)

- thinly sliced watermelon radishes
- thinly sliced cucumber
- crumbled feta cheese
- torn fresh mint
- fresh sprouts

BURGERS Wrap cucumber in clean tea towel and then squeeze to remove excess liquid. In small bowl, mix together cucumber, yogurt, harissa, honey and lemon juice.

In large bowl, mix together ¼ cup of the yogurt mixture, the chicken, garlic, egg, mint, coriander, cumin and salt.

Shape mixture into four ½-inch thick patties *(Make-ahead: Layer patties between parchment paper in airtight container; refrigerate for up to 24 hours.)*

Place patties on greased grill over medium-high heat; close lid and grill, turning once, until instant-read thermometer inserted sideways in patties reads 160°F, 8 to 10 minutes.

Place pitas on grill, turning once, until warmed through, about 1 minute. Spread some of the remaining yogurt mixture on pitas. Top pitas with patties. Add toppings (if using).

NUTRITIONAL INFORMATION PER SERVING about 414 cal, 30 g pro, 14 g total fat (4 g sat. fat), 40 g carb (3 g dietary fibre, 5 g sugar), 121 mg chol, 1,001 mg sodium, 468 mg potassium. % RDI: 18% calcium, 31% iron, 7% vit A, 8% vit C, 25% folate.

TIP FROM THE TEST KITCHEN

You can use ground beef or ground lamb in this recipe instead of chicken, if you prefer. To help keep patties from shrinking, make an indent in the centre of each with your thumb, about one-third of the way through, before grilling.

MAKES 4 SERVINGS
HANDS-ON TIME 20 MINUTES
TOTAL TIME 1¾ HOURS

Chicken, Olive & Lemon Tagine
With Dried Fruit Couscous

1 tsp	ground ginger
¾ tsp	cinnamon
¼ tsp	ground coriander
pinch	each nutmeg and cayenne pepper
2 tbsp	all-purpose flour
pinch	each salt and pepper
4	skin-on bone-in chicken thighs (about 650 g total)
4	skin-on chicken drumsticks (about 475 g total)
2 tsp	vegetable oil
1	onion, chopped
3	cloves garlic, chopped
2	carrots, sliced
1 cup	sodium-reduced chicken broth
2 tbsp	thinly sliced rinsed preserved lemon rind (see recipe, page 75)
1	bay leaf
½ cup	pitted green olives
2 tsp	lemon juice

DRIED FRUIT COUSCOUS

1 cup	couscous
¼ cup	dried apricots, chopped
¼ cup	golden raisins
¼ tsp	each salt and pepper
1½ cups	boiling water
1 tbsp	lemon juice
⅓ cup	chopped fresh cilantro

Stir together ginger, cinnamon, coriander, nutmeg and cayenne pepper; set aside half. Stir flour, salt and pepper into remainder. In large bowl, sprinkle flour mixture over chicken thighs and drumsticks; toss to coat. In Dutch oven or large heavy-bottomed ovenproof saucepan, heat oil over medium-high heat; brown chicken, in batches and turning once, about 4 minutes. Transfer to plate.

Drain all but 2 tsp fat from pan; cook onion over medium heat, stirring often, until softened and light golden, 5 minutes. Stir in garlic and carrots; cook until garlic is softened, 2 minutes. Stir in reserved ginger mixture; cook, stirring, until fragrant, 30 seconds. Stir in broth; bring to boil. Stir in preserved lemon rind and bay leaf; place chicken thighs (skin side up) and drumsticks over top.

Cover and braise in 350°F oven until chicken is tender and juices run clear when thickest part is pierced, about 1½ hours. Transfer chicken to platter; stir olives and lemon juice into pan. Spoon vegetable mixture and sauce around chicken on platter. Discard bay leaf.

DRIED FRUIT COUSCOUS Meanwhile, in bowl, stir together couscous, apricots, raisins, salt and pepper; pour boiling water and lemon juice over top. Cover and let stand until liquid is absorbed, about 5 minutes. Fluff with fork; stir in cilantro. Serve alongside chicken tagine.

NUTRITIONAL INFORMATION PER SERVING about 643 cal, 33 g pro, 33 g total fat (8 g sat. fat), 54 g carb (5 g dietary fibre, 13 g sugar), 130 mg chol, 733 mg sodium, 719 mg potassium. % RDI: 7% calcium, 23% iron, 73% vit A, 18% vit C, 20% folate.

Preserved Lemons

MAKES 2 JARS (EACH 2 CUPS)
HANDS-ON TIME 15 MINUTES
TOTAL TIME 1 MONTH

4	lemons
10 tbsp	coarse salt
1¼ cups	fresh lemon juice (not bottled)

Using brush, scrub lemons in bowl of warm, soapy water. Rinse well; pat dry.

Using paring knife, trim small tip of stem end from each lemon; quarter lemons.

Add 1 tbsp of the salt to each of two hot (sterilized) 2-cup jars with tight-fitting lids. Pack each jar with 4 lemon quarters, pushing down. Add another 1 tbsp of the salt and 4 lemon quarters to each jar, packing tightly. Divide remaining salt among jars; top each jar with enough lemon juice to cover. Seal tightly and shake gently to combine.

Refrigerate for at least 1 month. Store in refrigerator for up to 6 months. Rinse lemon pieces before using.

NUTRITIONAL INFORMATION PER 1 TSP about 3 cal, 0 g pro, trace total fat (0 g sat. fat), 1 g carb (1 g dietary fibre, trace sugar), 0 mg chol, 459 mg sodium, 19 mg potassium. % RDI: 1% calcium, 1% iron, 16% vit C.

TIP FROM THE TEST KITCHEN

Most recipes that call for preserved lemons only need the rind and not the soft pulp. Simply rinse the lemons to get rid of excess brine and scoop out the pulp with a spoon.

MAKES 4 SERVINGS
HANDS-ON TIME 30 MINUTES
TOTAL TIME 30 MINUTES

Spicy Fish & Chorizo Stew

2 tsp	olive oil
½ cup	diced dry-cured chorizo sausage
1	onion, diced
¼ tsp	hot pepper flakes
2 tbsp	tomato paste
4	cloves garlic, thinly sliced
1	can (796 mL) no-salt-added diced tomatoes
1	can (540 mL) no-salt-added white kidney beans, drained and rinsed
½ tsp	salt
340 g	skinless tilapia fillets or other white-fleshed fish, cut in 1-inch chunks
½ cup	chopped fresh cilantro
2 tsp	red wine vinegar

In large nonstick skillet, heat oil over medium heat; cook chorizo, stirring often, until lightly browned, about 3 minutes. Add onion and hot pepper flakes; cook, stirring occasionally, until onion is softened, about 5 minutes.

Stir in tomato paste and garlic; cook, stirring, until fragrant, about 1 minute. Add tomatoes; bring to boil. Reduce heat and simmer, stirring occasionally, until beginning to thicken, about 8 minutes.

Add beans and salt; cook, stirring occasionally, until heated through and stew is slightly thickened, about 5 minutes. Stir in fish; simmer until fish flakes easily when tested, about 2 minutes. Remove from heat; gently stir in cilantro and vinegar.

NUTRITIONAL INFORMATION PER SERVING about 376 cal, 32 g pro, 13 g total fat (4 g sat. fat), 34 g carb (9 g dietary fibre, 8 g sugar), 61 mg chol, 645 mg sodium, 1,248 mg potassium. % RDI: 10% calcium, 49% iron, 22% vit A, 25% vit C, 12% folate.

TIP FROM THE TEST KITCHEN

Check the label on your chorizo. The ones in the grocery store's deli department are already cured, so just need to be reheated. Fresh chorizo, available in some meat departments, needs to be cooked like any other fresh sausage.

Shrimp & Scallop Stew
With Lemony Orzo

MAKES 4 SERVINGS
HANDS-ON TIME 30 MINUTES
TOTAL TIME 30 MINUTES

SHRIMP & SCALLOP STEW In large nonstick skillet, heat oil over medium heat; cook leek, carrot and fennel, stirring occasionally, until softened and light golden, about 7 minutes. Stir in garlic, half each of the pepper and salt, the paprika, cumin and hot pepper flakes; cook, stirring, until fragrant, about 1 minute.

Stir in tomatoes and ½ cup water; bring to boil. Reduce heat and simmer, stirring occasionally, until thickened, 6 to 8 minutes.

Sprinkle shrimp and scallops with remaining pepper and salt. Stir into tomato mixture; cook, stirring occasionally, until shrimp are pink and scallops are opaque throughout, 5 to 7 minutes. Stir in parsley.

LEMONY ORZO Meanwhile, in large saucepan of boiling salted water, cook pasta according to package directions; drain. Stir in lemon zest and juice. Serve with stew.

NUTRITIONAL INFORMATION PER SERVING about 342 cal, 25 g pro, 5 g total fat (1 g sat. fat), 51 g carb (5 g dietary fibre, 10 g sugar), 73 mg chol, 345 mg sodium, 944 mg potassium. % RDI: 17% calcium, 31% iron, 52% vit A, 43% vit C, 57% folate.

SHRIMP & SCALLOP STEW

- **2 tsp** olive oil
- **1** leek (white and light green parts only), chopped
- **1** carrot, diced
- **half** bulb fennel, cored and chopped
- **3** cloves garlic, minced
- **½ tsp** pepper
- **¼ tsp** salt
- **¼ tsp** each smoked paprika and ground cumin
- **pinch** hot pepper flakes
- **1** can (796 mL) no-salt-added diced tomatoes
- **200 g** jumbo shrimp (21 to 25 count), peeled and deveined
- **200 g** sea scallops
- **2 tbsp** chopped fresh parsley

LEMONY ORZO

- **1 cup** orzo
- **½ tsp** grated lemon zest
- **1 tbsp** lemon juice

MAKES 4 SERVINGS
HANDS-ON TIME 6 MINUTES
TOTAL TIME 12 MINUTES

Prosciutto-Wrapped Grilled Fish

1 tsp chopped fresh thyme
¼ tsp pepper
4 white fish fillets, such as Pacific cod, catfish or tilapia (about 500 g total)
8 prosciutto slices (about 125 g total)
lemon wedges

Sprinkle thyme and pepper all over fish; wrap each fillet in prosciutto to almost cover. Secure with toothpick, if necessary.

Place on greased grill over medium-high heat; close lid and grill, turning once, until prosciutto is crispy and fish flakes easily when tested, about 6 minutes. Serve with lemon wedges.

NUTRITIONAL INFORMATION PER SERVING about 140 cal, 25 g pro, 3 g total fat (1 g sat. fat), 1 g carb, 64 mg chol, 431 mg sodium. % RDI: 1% calcium, 6% iron, 1% vit A, 2% vit C, 5% folate.

MAKES 8 SERVINGS
HANDS-ON TIME 5 MINUTES
TOTAL TIME 15 MINUTES

Greek-Style Grilled Fish

1.5 kg pickerel fillets, skin on
⅓ cup extra-virgin olive oil
1 tbsp minced fresh oregano
1 tsp each sea salt and pepper
2 tbsp capers, drained and rinsed
1 lemon, cut in wedges
1 bunch watercress (or purslane)

Brush fillets with half of the oil. Sprinkle with oregano, salt and pepper.

Place, skin side down, on greased grill over medium heat; close lid and grill, without turning, until fish flakes easily when tested, about 10 minutes. Transfer to platter.

Drizzle with remaining oil; sprinkle with capers. Surround with lemon and watercress.

NUTRITIONAL INFORMATION PER SERVING about 223 cal, 29 g pro, 11 g total fat (2 g sat. fat), 1 g carb (trace dietary fibre), 129 mg chol, 340 mg sodium. % RDI: 17% calcium, 16% iron, 9% vit A, 13% vit C, 10% folate.

Mussels in Tomato Saffron Broth

MAKES 4 SERVINGS
HANDS-ON TIME 8 MINUTES
TOTAL TIME 25 MINUTES

½ cup	dry white wine
pinch	saffron threads, crumbled
900 g	fresh mussels
1	can (796 mL) plum tomatoes
¼ cup	extra-virgin olive oil
half	Spanish onion, chopped
1	clove garlic, minced
3 tbsp	ground almonds
1	jarred roasted red pepper, chopped
¼ cup	chopped fresh flatleaf parsley
pinch	salt

Stir wine with saffron; let stand for at least 10 or up to 20 minutes.

Scrub mussels and remove any beards. Discard any that do not close when tapped. Set aside.

Reserving liquid, drain tomatoes; seed and coarsely chop. Set aside.

In large saucepan, heat oil over medium heat; cook onion and garlic, stirring occasionally, until onion is softened, about 6 minutes. Add almonds; cook for 1 minute. Add red pepper, tomatoes, ½ cup of the reserved tomato liquid, the saffron mixture, half of the parsley and the salt; bring to boil. Reduce heat to low; simmer until slightly thickened, about 10 minutes.

Add mussels; cover and simmer until mussels open, about 5 minutes. Discard any that do not open. Remove from heat. Sprinkle with remaining parsley.

NUTRITIONAL INFORMATION PER SERVING about 260 cal, 11 g pro, 18 g total fat (2 g sat. fat), 15 g carb, 3 g dietary fibre, 19 mg chol, 295 mg sodium. % RDI: 7% calcium, 31% iron, 14% vit A, 100% vit C, 22% folate.

TIP FROM THE TEST KITCHEN

Saffron is an expensive spice, but you only need a tiny quantity to add rich golden colour and earthy flavour. Soaking saffron threads in a small quantity of liquid before cooking helps distribute the colour and flavour evenly through the dish.

MAKES 4 SERVINGS
HANDS-ON TIME 18 MINUTES
TOTAL TIME 25 MINUTES

Mussels in Harissa Broth

900 g	fresh mussels
1 tbsp	butter
3	shallots, diced
3	cloves garlic, minced
¾ cup	white wine
1 cup	clam juice or sodium-reduced chicken broth
1 tsp	harissa paste
2 tbsp	chopped fresh parsley

Scrub mussels and remove any beards. Discard any that do not close when tapped. Set aside.

In large skillet, melt butter over medium heat; cook shallots, stirring occasionally, until softened, about 5 minutes. Add garlic; cook until fragrant, about 2 minutes.

Add wine; simmer until reduced by half, about 5 minutes. Stir in clam juice and harissa; return to boil.

Add mussels; cover with tight-fitting lid and simmer until mussels open, about 5 minutes. Discard any that do not open. Remove from heat. Toss with parsley.

NUTRITIONAL INFORMATION PER SERVING about 118 cal, 9 g pro, 5 g total fat (2 g sat. fat), 5 g carb (trace dietary fibre, 1 g sugar), 28 mg chol, 291 mg sodium, 274 mg potassium. % RDI: 3% calcium, 21% iron, 10% vit A, 13% vit C, 15% folate.

TIP FROM THE TEST KITCHEN

Look for small jars or tubes of harissa (Tunisia's fiery blend of chilies, cumin, coriander and garlic) in Middle Eastern grocery stores and some supermarkets.

Charred Shrimp & Cauliflower Romesco

MAKES 4 SERVINGS
HANDS-ON TIME 30 MINUTES
TOTAL TIME 30 MINUTES

ROMESCO SAUCE

1	jar (300 mL) roasted red peppers, including juices
¼ cup	prepared tomato sauce
3 tbsp	almond butter
2 tsp	red wine vinegar
1 tsp	smoked paprika
¼ tsp	cayenne pepper

SHRIMP & VEGETABLES

1	head cauliflower, cut in large florets
¼ tsp	salt
1	bunch green onions
450 g	unpeeled jumbo shrimp (21 to 25 count)
1 tbsp	vegetable oil

ROMESCO SAUCE In blender, purée together red peppers including juices, tomato sauce, almond butter, vinegar, paprika and cayenne pepper until smooth. Transfer to microwaveable bowl; set aside.

SHRIMP & VEGETABLES Place cauliflower in microwaveable baking dish. Add 1 tbsp water and pinch of salt; toss to coat. Cover with plastic wrap; poke 1 hole to vent steam. Microwave on high for 5 minutes.

Trim roots and dark green tops of green onions. Set aside.

In bowl, toss together shrimp, oil and remaining salt.

Thread shrimp onto metal or soaked wooden skewers. Place shrimp and cauliflower on greased grill over medium-high heat; close lid and grill, turning once, until shrimp are pink and cauliflower is charred, about 8 minutes. Add green onions during last 3 minutes of grilling.

Microwave Romesco Sauce on high, stirring every 30 seconds, until warm, 1 to 2 minutes. Serve cauliflower, shrimp and green onions on large platter with sauce on the side for dipping.

NUTRITIONAL INFORMATION PER SERVING about 245 cal, 22 g pro, 13 g total fat (1 g sat. fat), 14 g carb (5 g dietary fibre, 6 g sugar), 128 mg chol, 714 mg sodium, 606 mg potassium. % RDI: 10% calcium, 26% iron, 32% vit A, 283% vit C, 33% folate.

TIP FROM THE TEST KITCHEN

If you can find only large jars of roasted red peppers, consider making a double batch of Romesco Sauce. It freezes very well and pairs amazingly with beef, chicken, white fish and grilled vegetables.

MAKES 6 SERVINGS
HANDS-ON TIME 15 MINUTES
TOTAL TIME 30 MINUTES

Piri-Piri Shrimp & Chorizo Kabobs

24	mini yellow-fleshed potatoes
¼ cup	piri-piri spice rub
2 tbsp	olive oil
2 tbsp	liquid honey
1 tbsp	warm water (approx)
24	jumbo shrimp (21 to 25 count), peeled and deveined
1	small red onion, cut in 1-inch pieces
1	chorizo sausage, sliced in 24 rounds
3 tbsp	chopped fresh chives (optional)
2	limes, cut in wedges

In microwaveable dish, cover and microwave potatoes on high until tender, 5 to 8 minutes. Let cool slightly.

Meanwhile, in large bowl, mix piri-piri spice rub with oil. Spoon 1 tbsp of piri-piri mixture into small bowl; stir in honey and up to 1 tbsp warm water to make glaze; set aside.

Add cooled potatoes to large bowl with piri-piri mixture. Add shrimp; toss to coat. *(Make-ahead: Cover and refrigerate for up to 24 hours.)* Alternately thread shrimp, potato, red onion and chorizo onto 12 metal or soaked wooden skewers.

Place kabobs on greased grill over medium-high heat; close lid and grill, turning once, until shrimp are pink, 4 to 5 minutes. Brush with reserved piri-piri glaze; sprinkle with chives (if using). Serve with lime wedges.

NUTRITIONAL INFORMATION PER SERVING about 420 cal, 27 g pro, 24 g total fat (8 g sat. fat), 24 g carb (2 g dietary fibre, 8 g sugar), 149 mg chol, 876 mg sodium, 735 mg potassium. % RDI: 6% calcium, 28% iron, 16% vit A, 18% vit C, 11% folate.

TIP FROM THE TEST KITCHEN

Piri-piri spice rub is a Portuguese blend with African roots and a fiery kick. If you prefer less heat than you'll find in most store-bought blends, substitute with ¼ cup of our mild piri-piri blend. Stir together ¼ cup sweet paprika; 2 tbsp each smoked paprika, ground cumin and ground coriander; 2 tsp each garlic powder, onion powder and packed brown sugar; and 1 tsp each salt and pepper. *(Make-ahead: Store in airtight container for up to 2 weeks.)*

Cacio e Pepe

MAKES 4 SERVINGS
HANDS-ON TIME 15 MINUTES
TOTAL TIME 30 MINUTES

1	batch Fresh Pasta Dough (see recipe, page 88)
½ cup	all-purpose flour (approx)
2 tbsp	olive oil
¾ tsp	pepper
1⅓ cups	finely shredded Pecorino-Romano or Parmesan cheese

With pasta machine roller on widest setting and working with 1 sheet at a time, feed dough through lightly floured rollers. Fold dough in half, bringing short ends together; lightly dust dough with some flour. Feed dough through rollers 3 more times or until edges are smooth, cutting in half if too long to handle; continue feeding through rollers, reducing the setting as you go, until third-widest setting (about 3 mm) is reached.

Lightly dust dough with some of the remaining flour. Working with 1 sheet at a time, fold dough in half, bringing short ends together; repeat twice to create 8-layer stack. Using sharp knife, cut crosswise into ⅛-inch thick strips. Using hands, separate pasta; dust generously with remaining flour. On lightly floured baking sheet, shape pasta into nests. Let stand until leathery but not dry, about 10 minutes. *(Make-ahead: Freeze until firm; transfer to resealable freezer bag and freeze for up to 3 weeks.)*

Gently separate pasta, removing excess flour. In large saucepan of boiling salted water, cook pasta until al dente, about 4 minutes. Reserving ¾ cup of the cooking liquid, drain.

In same pan, heat oil with pepper over medium heat; stir in pasta, 1 cup of the Pecorino-Romano and enough of the reserved cooking liquid to coat. Sprinkle with remaining Pecorino-Romano.

NUTRITIONAL INFORMATION PER SERVING about 469 cal, 23 g pro, 21 g total fat (8 g sat. fat), 45 g carb (2 g dietary fibre, 1 g sugar), 179 mg chol, 952 mg sodium, 139 mg potassium. % RDI: 35% calcium, 28% iron, 12% vit A, 51% folate.

VARIATION

Aglio e Olio

Omit pepper and Pecorino-Romano cheese. Add 4 cloves garlic, sliced, and pinch hot pepper flakes to olive oil. Cook as directed. Sprinkle with 2 tbsp chopped fresh parsley.

MAKES 1 BATCH DOUGH
HANDS-ON TIME 15 MINUTES
TOTAL TIME 35 MINUTES

Fresh Pasta Dough

2 cups all-purpose flour
3 large eggs
¼ tsp salt

Mound flour on work surface; make well in centre. Crack eggs into well; sprinkle with salt. Using fork, beat eggs. Starting at inside edge and working around well, gradually stir flour into egg mixture until soft dough forms. Sift flour remaining on work surface; discard any bits of dough.

On lightly floured work surface, knead dough, dusting with some of the reserved flour, until dough is smooth, elastic and no longer sticky, about 10 minutes. Shape into disc; wrap in plastic wrap. Let stand for 20 minutes.

Cut dough into thirds; roll or press each into 5-inch wide sheet. Dust with reserved flour. Cover with damp towel (to prevent drying out).

Fresh Tomato Sauce

MAKES ABOUT 11 CUPS
HANDS-ON TIME 30 MINUTES
TOTAL TIME 2 HOURS

4 kg	plum tomatoes (about 40)
2	onions, chopped
½ cup	olive oil
3	cloves garlic, minced
1	can (156 mL) tomato paste
1¼ tsp	salt
½ tsp	pepper

Score an X in bottom of each tomato. In large saucepan of boiling water, cook tomatoes until skins begin to loosen, about 1 minute. Using slotted spoon, transfer to bowl of ice water and chill for 20 seconds; drain.

Working over fine-mesh sieve set over bowl, peel off tomato skins; discard. Reserving 3 cups of juices, core tomatoes and transfer seeds to sieve; press seeds to extract juices. Set juices aside. Discard seeds and cores.

In food processor, purée tomato flesh, in batches, until smooth. (Purée should yield approximately 10 cups.) Scrape into bowl. Set aside.

In food processor, purée onions until smooth.

In Dutch oven or large heavy-bottomed saucepan, heat oil over medium heat; cook onions, stirring occasionally, until golden and liquid has evaporated, about 12 minutes. Stir in garlic; cook, stirring, until fragrant, about 1 minute. Stir in tomato purée, reserved tomato juice, tomato paste, salt and pepper. Bring to boil; reduce heat and simmer, uncovered, stirring occasionally, until sauce has reduced to about 11 cups, about 1½ hours. *(Make-ahead: Let cool; refrigerate in airtight container for up to 1 week or freeze for up to 2 months.)*

NUTRITIONAL INFORMATION PER ½ CUP about 80 cal, 2 g pro, 5 g total fat (1 g sat. fat), 8 g carb (2 g dietary fibre, 5 g sugar), 0 mg chol, 146 mg sodium, 429 mg potassium. % RDI: 2% calcium, 5% iron, 12% vit A, 32% vit C, 8% folate.

VARIATION

Pressure Cooker Fresh Tomato Sauce

Follow first 4 paragraphs as directed. In pressure cooker, heat oil over medium heat; cook onions and garlic as directed.

Stir in tomato purée, 2 cups of the reserved tomato juice, the tomato paste, salt and pepper. (Reserve remaining tomato juice for another use.) Secure lid; bring to high pressure over high heat. Reduce heat while maintaining high pressure; cook for 20 minutes. Remove from heat; let pressure release completely, about 2 minutes.

MAKES 6 SERVINGS
HANDS-ON TIME 10 MINUTES
TOTAL TIME 20 MINUTES

Pot Roast Pasta Ragù

1	can (796 mL) whole plum tomatoes, drained
4 cups	shredded Hearty Italian Pot Roast (see recipe, page 34)
2 cups	sauce from Hearty Italian Pot Roast (see recipe, page 34)
1 tsp	Italian herb seasoning
1	pkg (454 g) ziti tagliati
1 cup	loosely packed fresh basil leaves (approx)
½ cup	grated pecorino or Parmesan cheese (approx)

Using hands, crush tomatoes. In large saucepan over medium heat, stir together tomatoes, Hearty Italian Pot Roast, pot roast sauce and Italian seasoning. Cook, stirring occasionally, until heated through, 10 to 15 minutes.

Meanwhile, in large saucepan of boiling salted water, cook pasta according to package directions. Drain; return to saucepan.

Add sauce to pan with pasta; stir in basil and pecorino. Cover and let stand for 5 minutes. Garnish with more basil and pecorino, if desired.

NUTRITIONAL INFORMATION PER SERVING about 510 cal, 38 g pro, 9 g total fat (4 g sat. fat), 66 g carb (4 g dietary fibre, 5 g sugar), 61 mg chol, 680 mg sodium, 776 mg potassium. % RDI: 8% calcium, 46% iron, 19% vit A, 30% vit C, 85% folate.

MAKES 6 SERVINGS
HANDS-ON TIME 10 MINUTES
TOTAL TIME 40 MINUTES

Easy Spaghetti Sauce

In saucepan, heat 2 tbsp vegetable oil over medium heat. Add 1 small onion, chopped; 1 carrot, diced; 1 stalk celery, diced; 1 sweet green pepper, diced; ¾ tsp each salt and dried basil; and pinch hot pepper flakes. Cook, stirring occasionally, until onion is softened, about 8 minutes.

Add ¼ cup tomato paste and 1 can (796 mL) diced tomatoes; bring to boil. Reduce heat and simmer, uncovered, until thickened, about 30 minutes. *(Make-ahead: Let cool. Cover and refrigerate for up to 2 days or freeze for up to 2 months.)*

NUTRITIONAL INFORMATION PER SERVING about 91 cal, 2 g pro, 5 g total fat (trace sat. fat), 12 g carb (2 g dietary fibre), 0 mg chol, 506 mg sodium. % RDI: 5% calcium, 9% iron, 42% vit A, 63% vit C, 8% folate.

Pot Roast Pasta Ragù

Rigatoni Alfredo
With Chicken & Zucchini

MAKES 6 SERVINGS
HANDS-ON TIME 25 MINUTES
TOTAL TIME 30 MINUTES

375 g	rigatoni
1 tbsp	olive oil
4	boneless skinless chicken thighs, cut in ½-inch wide strips
¼ tsp	salt
2	small yellow or green zucchini, thinly sliced crosswise
2 tsp	grated lemon zest
2 tbsp	lemon juice
1 cup	finely grated Parmesan cheese
1 cup	whipping cream (35%)
2 tbsp	chopped fresh thyme
½ tsp	pepper

In large saucepan of boiling salted water, cook pasta according to package directions. Reserving ½ cup of the cooking liquid, drain.

Meanwhile, in large skillet, heat oil over medium heat. Add chicken and salt; cook, stirring occasionally, until browned, 3 to 4 minutes. Add zucchini; cook, stirring occasionally, until softened, about 2 minutes. Transfer to bowl; set aside.

In same skillet, add lemon juice; cook, scraping up any browned bits, for 1 to 2 minutes. Add Parmesan, cream, thyme and pepper; cook, stirring frequently, until slightly thickened, 3 to 4 minutes. Stir in pasta, chicken and zucchini. If needed, add reserved cooking liquid, 1 tbsp at a time, to loosen sauce. Stir in lemon zest. Serve immediately.

NUTRITIONAL INFORMATION PER SERVING about 539 cal, 27 g pro, 25 g total fat (13 g sat. fat), 51 g carb (3 g dietary fibre, 2 g sugar), 109 mg chol, 609 mg sodium, 430 mg potassium. % RDI: 22% calcium, 22% iron, 24% vit A, 23% vit C, 75% folate.

TIP FROM THE TEST KITCHEN

For those who prefer more spice, stir in ½ tsp hot pepper flakes and a couple of pressed or finely grated garlic cloves with the lemon juice.

MAKES ABOUT 7 CUPS
HANDS-ON TIME 15 MINUTES
TOTAL TIME 1½ HOURS

Smoky Pork Bolognese Sauce

450 g	lean ground pork
2	strips bacon, chopped
2	carrots, diced
2	stalks celery, diced
1	onion, diced
3	cloves garlic, minced
4 cups	Fresh Tomato Sauce (see recipe, page 99) or good-quality plain tomato sauce
1 cup	dry red wine
1 tsp	granulated sugar
1 tsp	dried oregano
¼ tsp	hot pepper flakes
1	bay leaf
¼ cup	chopped fresh parsley

In Dutch oven or large heavy-bottomed saucepan, cook pork and bacon over medium-high heat, breaking up pork with spoon, until no longer pink, about 7 minutes. Using slotted spoon, transfer to bowl. Set aside. Drain all but 2 tbsp fat from pan.

Add carrots, celery and onion to pan; cook over medium heat, stirring occasionally, until softened, about 10 minutes. Add garlic; cook, stirring, until fragrant, about 1 minute.

Stir in pork mixture, tomato sauce, wine, sugar, oregano, hot pepper flakes and bay leaf. Bring to boil; reduce heat, cover and simmer, stirring occasionally, until slightly thickened, about 1 hour. Discard bay leaf. Stir in parsley. *(Make-ahead: Let cool; refrigerate in airtight container for up to 2 days or freeze for up to 2 months.)*

NUTRITIONAL INFORMATION PER ½ CUP about 135 cal, 8 g pro, 8 g total fat (2 g sat. fat), 8 g carb (2 g dietary fibre, 4 g sugar), 22 mg chol, 148 mg sodium, 433 mg potassium. % RDI: 3% calcium, 7% iron, 27% vit A, 23% vit C, 8% folate.

TIP FROM THE TEST KITCHEN

This sauce freezes well, making for quick weeknight dinners. Simply reheat and serve over the hot cooked pasta of your choice.

Crab, Pea & Ricotta Spaghetti

MAKES 4 TO 6 SERVINGS
HANDS-ON TIME 15 MINUTES
TOTAL TIME 25 MINUTES

375 g	spaghetti
1 cup	fresh or frozen peas
1 cup	smooth ricotta cheese
2 tbsp	finely chopped fresh tarragon (approx)
2 tbsp	olive oil
2 tbsp	butter, softened
2 tsp	grated lemon zest
1 tbsp	lemon juice
half	Thai bird's-eye pepper, seeded and minced (approx)
½ tsp	salt
¼ tsp	pepper
pinch	nutmeg
1½ cups	shredded cooked crabmeat

In large saucepan of boiling salted water, cook pasta according to package directions, adding peas during last 2 minutes of cooking. Reserving 1 cup of the cooking liquid, drain. Return pasta mixture to pan over medium-low heat.

Stir in ricotta, tarragon, oil, butter, lemon zest, lemon juice, Thai pepper, salt, pepper, nutmeg and enough of the reserved cooking liquid to loosen sauce; fold in crabmeat. Stir in up to 1 tbsp more tarragon and half Thai pepper, seeded and minced, if you wish. Cook until warmed through, about 3 minutes.

NUTRITIONAL INFORMATION PER EACH OF 6 SERVINGS about 457 cal, 26 g pro, 16 g total fat (7 g sat. fat), 52 g carb (3 g dietary fibre, 2 g sugar), 69 mg chol, 768 mg sodium, 348 mg potassium. % RDI: 12% calcium, 19% iron, 14% vit A, 10% vit C, 82% folate.

TIP FROM THE TEST KITCHEN

Tossing this dish with some of the pasta cooking liquid helps distribute the sauce evenly and adds creaminess without using extra oil or butter.

MAKES 2 TO 3 SERVINGS
HANDS-ON TIME 15 MINUTES
TOTAL TIME 20 MINUTES

Lemony Ravioli With Sun-Dried Tomatoes

250 g	fresh vegetable- or cheese-filled ravioli
1 tbsp	each butter and olive oil
¼ cup	thinly sliced drained oil-packed sun-dried tomatoes
2	cloves garlic, minced
¼ cup	each finely grated Parmesan cheese and chopped fresh parsley
1 tbsp	thinly sliced lemon zest
3 tbsp	lemon juice
1 tbsp	capers, drained and rinsed

In saucepan of boiling salted water, cook pasta according to package directions. Reserving ⅓ cup of the cooking liquid, drain.

In large nonstick skillet, heat butter and oil over medium heat until melted; cook sun-dried tomatoes and garlic, stirring often, until fragrant, 2 to 3 minutes. Add pasta, Parmesan, parsley, lemon zest, lemon juice and capers; cook, stirring gently, for 2 minutes. Stir in enough of the reserved cooking liquid to coat.

NUTRITIONAL INFORMATION PER EACH OF 3 SERVINGS about 322 cal, 10 g pro, 18 g total fat (6 g sat. fat), 32 g carb (3 g dietary fibre, 3 g sugar), 39 mg chol, 779 mg sodium, 211 mg potassium. % RDI: 14% calcium, 18% iron, 9% vit A, 35% vit C, 5% folate.

MAKES 1 CUP
HANDS-ON TIME 5 MINUTES
TOTAL TIME 5 MINUTES

Sun-Dried Tomato & Almond Pesto

In food processor, pulse ½ cup slivered almonds with 2 cloves garlic until coarsely ground. Add 1 cup drained oil-packed sun-dried tomatoes and ¼ tsp each salt and pepper; pulse until finely chopped. With motor running, add ⅓ cup extra-virgin olive oil in thin steady stream until smooth. *(Make-ahead: Refrigerate in airtight container for up to 3 days or freeze for up to 6 months.)*

NUTRITIONAL INFORMATION PER 1 TBSP about 75 cal, 1 g pro, 7 g total fat (1 g sat. fat), 2 g carb (1 g dietary fibre, 1 g sugar), 0 mg chol, 55 mg sodium, 133 mg potassium. % RDI: 1% calcium, 3% iron, 1% vit A, 12% vit C, 1% folate.

Lemony Ravioli
With Sun-Dried Tomatoes

Chorizo & Jerusalem Artichoke Penne

MAKES 4 SERVINGS
HANDS-ON TIME 25 MINUTES
TOTAL TIME 25 MINUTES

340 g	penne
⅓ cup	thinly sliced dry-cured chorizo sausage
450 g	Jerusalem artichokes, peeled and cut in ¼-inch thick slices
3	cloves garlic, thinly sliced
1½ tsp	chopped fresh thyme
1 tsp	olive oil
4 cups	lightly packed baby spinach
⅓ cup	whipping cream (35%)
½ tsp	grated lemon zest
4 tsp	lemon juice
¼ tsp	each salt and pepper
¼ cup	finely grated Parmesan cheese

In large saucepan of boiling lightly salted water, cook pasta according to package directions. Reserving ½ cup of the cooking liquid, drain. Set aside.

While pasta is cooking, in large nonstick skillet, cook chorizo over medium-high heat, stirring occasionally, until lightly browned and crisp, about 2 minutes. Using slotted spoon, transfer to plate. Set aside.

In same skillet, cook artichokes over medium heat, stirring occasionally, until beginning to brown, about 5 minutes. Stir in ⅓ cup water; cover and simmer until artichokes are fork-tender and most of the liquid has evaporated, 5 to 7 minutes.

Add garlic, thyme and oil; cook, stirring, until fragrant, about 1 minute. Add spinach; cook, stirring, until wilted, about 1 minute. Stir in pasta, cream and enough of the reserved cooking liquid to coat. Remove from heat. Stir in lemon zest, lemon juice, salt and pepper. Sprinkle with chorizo and Parmesan.

NUTRITIONAL INFORMATION PER SERVING about 561 cal, 21 g pro, 16 g total fat (8 g sat. fat), 83 g carb (5 g dietary fibre, 10 g sugar), 41 mg chol, 743 mg sodium, 752 mg potassium. % RDI: 15% calcium, 54% iron, 50% vit A, 17% vit C, 119% folate.

TIP FROM THE TEST KITCHEN

Jerusalem artichokes, or sunchokes, have a subtle flavour and a texture somewhere between that of a potato and a water chestnut. Use a vegetable peeler to remove their skins; rinse to remove any grit, if necessary, and pat dry.

MAKES 4 SERVINGS
HANDS-ON TIME 15 MINUTES
TOTAL TIME 15 MINUTES

Penne With Anchovies & Rosemary Cream Sauce

340 g	penne
2 tsp	olive oil
4	cloves garlic, thinly sliced
6	oil-packed anchovy fillets, mashed
¾ cup	sodium-reduced chicken broth
½ cup	whipping cream (35%)
4 tsp	chopped fresh rosemary
2 tsp	Dijon mustard
¼ tsp	pepper
¼ tsp	hot pepper flakes
1¼ cups	frozen peas
¾ cup	jarred roasted red peppers, drained and coarsely chopped
1 tbsp	capers, drained, rinsed and chopped

In large saucepan of boiling salted water, cook pasta according to package directions. Reserving ½ cup of the cooking liquid, drain.

Meanwhile, in large nonstick skillet, heat oil over medium heat; cook garlic, stirring, until golden, about 4 minutes. Add anchovies; cook, stirring, for 1 minute. Whisk in broth, cream, 1 tbsp of the rosemary, the mustard, pepper and hot pepper flakes; cook until slightly thickened, about 4 minutes.

Stir in peas; cook until heated through. Stir in pasta, red peppers and capers. If needed, gradually stir in enough of the reserved cooking liquid to loosen sauce. Sprinkle with remaining rosemary.

NUTRITIONAL INFORMATION PER SERVING about 182 cal, 6 g pro, 14 g total fat (7 g sat. fat), 11 g carb (3 g dietary fibre, 4 g sugar), 43 mg chol, 669 mg sodium, 189 mg potassium. % RDI: 6% calcium, 9% iron, 30% vit A, 120% vit C, 15% folate.

TIP FROM THE TEST KITCHEN

Anchovies melt seamlessly into cream sauces, adding savoury flavour without any of the fishiness you might expect. They're also loaded with protein, calcium and omega-3 fatty acids.

Quick Baked Ziti
With Sausage & Mushrooms

MAKES 4 TO 6 SERVINGS
HANDS-ON TIME 25 MINUTES
TOTAL TIME 35 MINUTES

400 g	mild Italian sausage, casings removed
1 tsp	olive oil
1	onion, chopped
1	pkg (227 g) cremini mushrooms, sliced
3	cloves garlic, minced
1 tsp	Italian herb seasoning
¼ tsp	hot pepper flakes
1	bottle (680 mL) strained tomatoes (passata)
400 g	ziti or penne
¼ cup	chopped fresh basil
3 tbsp	chopped fresh parsley
1 cup	shredded part-skim mozzarella cheese

In Dutch oven or large heavy-bottomed saucepan, cook sausage over medium heat, breaking up with spoon, until no longer pink, about 5 minutes. Using slotted spoon, transfer to plate. Set aside.

Drain fat from pan. Add oil; cook onion and mushrooms over medium heat, stirring often and scraping up any browned bits with wooden spoon, until softened and no liquid remains, about 6 minutes. Add garlic, Italian seasoning and hot pepper flakes; cook, stirring, until fragrant, about 1 minute. Stir in sausage and passata; bring to boil. Reduce heat and simmer, stirring, until slightly thickened, about 4 minutes.

Meanwhile, in large saucepan of boiling lightly salted water, cook pasta until slightly undercooked, about 2 minutes less than package directions. Reserving ½ cup of the cooking liquid, drain. Stir pasta, 3 tbsp of the basil, 2 tbsp of the parsley and reserved cooking liquid into sauce; cook, stirring until slightly thickened, about 1 minute.

Scrape into lightly greased 8-cup casserole dish. Sprinkle with mozzarella. Bake in 400°F oven until cheese is melted, about 3 minutes. Broil until cheese is golden and bubbly, about 2 minutes. Let stand for 5 minutes. Sprinkle with remaining basil and parsley.

NUTRITIONAL INFORMATION PER EACH OF 6 SERVINGS about 515 cal, 26 g pro, 19 g total fat (6 g sat. fat), 60 g carb (4 g dietary fibre, 6 g sugar), 43 mg chol, 858 mg sodium, 477 mg potassium. % RDI: 17% calcium, 26% iron, 6% vit A, 22% vit C, 75% folate.

TIP FROM THE TEST KITCHEN

For easy shredding, freeze the mozzarella for a few minutes first.

MAKES 4 SERVINGS
HANDS-ON TIME 15 MINUTES
TOTAL TIME 25 MINUTES

Lazy Veggie Skillet Lasagna

6	lasagna noodles
¼ cup	fresh basil
½ cup	ricotta cheese
1 tbsp	olive oil
2	zucchini
1	carrot
2 cups	jarred pasta sauce
1 cup	shredded mozzarella cheese

Break lasagna noodles into thirds. In large saucepan of boiling salted water, cook noodles according to package directions until al dente, 7 to 9 minutes; drain. Meanwhile, chop half of the basil; stir with ricotta. Set aside.

In cast-iron or ovenproof skillet, heat oil over medium heat. Using vegetable peeler, slice zucchini and carrot lengthwise into long ribbons; cook until tender, 3 to 5 minutes. Add noodles and pasta sauce; simmer, stirring occasionally, until warm, about 3 minutes.

Sprinkle with mozzarella; dollop with ricotta mixture. Bake in 475°F oven until mozzarella is melted, 7 to 10 minutes. Tear remaining basil into small pieces; sprinkle over top.

NUTRITIONAL INFORMATION PER SERVING about 440 cal, 17 g pro, 19 g total fat (8 g sat. fat), 51 g carb (6 g dietary fibre, 15 g sugar), 43 mg chol, 675 mg sodium, 709 mg potassium. % RDI: 26% calcium, 14% iron, 79% vit A, 18% vit C, 20% folate.

VARIATION

Lazy Zucchini & Carrot Skillet

Omit lasagna noodles; double the quantity of zucchini and carrot.

Speedy Mini Lasagnas

MAKES 4 SERVINGS
HANDS-ON TIME 20 MINUTES
TOTAL TIME 30 MINUTES

8	lasagna noodles, broken in bite-size pieces
2 tsp	olive oil
300 g	extra-lean ground beef
1	onion, diced
3	cloves garlic, pressed or finely grated
1 tbsp	Italian herb seasoning
½ tsp	salt
¼ tsp	pepper
1	small zucchini (peel-on), grated
1	bottle (680 mL) strained tomatoes (passata)
4 tsp	liquid honey
⅔ cup	extra-smooth ricotta cheese
½ cup	finely grated Parmesan cheese
½ cup	chopped fresh basil
1	egg yolk
½ cup	shredded mozzarella cheese

In large saucepan of boiling lightly salted water, cook noodles according to package directions until al dente. Drain.

Meanwhile, in large skillet, heat oil over medium-high heat; cook beef, onion, two-thirds of the garlic, the Italian seasoning, salt and pepper, stirring occasionally and breaking up beef with spoon, until beef is no longer pink and onion is softened, about 5 minutes.

Add zucchini; cook, stirring, until softened, about 2 minutes. Reduce heat to medium. Add passata and honey; cook, stirring, until hot and combined, about 1 minute. Stir in noodles. Spoon into four 1½-cup ramekins.

In bowl, stir together ricotta, Parmesan, basil, egg yolk and remaining garlic until smooth. Spoon over noodle mixture, spreading to edges of ramekins. Sprinkle with mozzarella.

Broil on rimmed baking sheet on centre rack until tops are browned and bubbly, 3 to 4 minutes. Let stand for 5 minutes before serving.

NUTRITIONAL INFORMATION PER SERVING about 587 cal, 38 g pro, 22 g total fat (11 g sat. fat), 57 g carb (5 g dietary fibre, 12 g sugar), 125 mg chol, 827 mg sodium, 495 mg potassium. % RDI: 32% calcium, 36% iron, 53% vit A, 12% vit C, 63% folate.

TIP FROM THE TEST KITCHEN

Broiling the lasagnas on the centre rack allows the ricotta mixture to become hot and bubbly before the tops brown.

MAKES 4 SERVINGS
HANDS-ON TIME 10 MINUTES
TOTAL TIME 30 MINUTES

Couscous & Green Pea Falafel Plate

TAHINI DRESSING

3 tbsp each tahini and Balkan-style yogurt
2 tsp each lemon juice and liquid honey
¼ tsp salt

FALAFELS

½ cup couscous
¾ cup boiling water
5 tbsp Balkan-style yogurt
1 tbsp tahini
1 cup frozen peas, thawed and drained
1 cup fresh cilantro leaves and stems, torn
1 cup fresh parsley leaves and stems, torn
4 green onions, sliced, white and green parts separated
2 tbsp all purpose flour
2 tsp lemon zest
¾ tsp salt
2 tbsp vegetable oil

KALE & SPINACH SALAD

4 cups kale, torn
4 cups baby spinach
8 cocktail tomatoes, quartered
half English cucumber, cut in half moons
3 tbsp unsalted roasted sunflower seeds
pinch cayenne pepper (optional)

TAHINI DRESSING Whisk together tahini, yogurt, 3 tbsp water, lemon juice, honey and salt. Set aside.

FALAFELS In medium bowl, stir together couscous and boiling water; cover and let stand for 5 minutes. Uncover and fluff with fork.

Place half of the couscous, the remaining yogurt and tahini, the peas, cilantro, parsley, white parts of green onions, flour, lemon zest and salt in food processor; pulse until coarsely ground. Transfer to bowl with remaining couscous and mix to combine. Using damp hands, shape mixture into 12 equal patties. In a large skillet, heat 1 tbsp oil over medium heat; working in batches and turning halfway through, cook falafels until golden, about 8 minutes. Repeat with remaining falafels, adding more oil as needed.

KALE & SPINACH SALAD Divide kale, spinach, tomatoes, cucumbers, green parts of green onions and sunflower seeds between 4 serving plates. Place 3 falafels on each plate; drizzle with tahini dressing and sprinkle with cayenne (if using).

NUTRITIONAL INFORMATION PER SERVING about 420 cal, 15 g pro, 21 g total fat (8 g sat. fat), 49 g carb (9 g dietary fibre, 7 g sugar), 5 mg chol, 741 mg sodium, 870 mg potassium. % RDI: 29% calcium, 38% iron, 330% vit A, 233% vit C, 30% folate.

Moroccan Vegetable Couscous

MAKES 6 SERVINGS
HANDS-ON TIME 20 MINUTES
TOTAL TIME 40 MINUTES

1 tbsp	olive oil
2	cloves garlic, minced
2 tsp	minced fresh ginger
1	small onion, sliced
1 tsp	each ground coriander and turmeric
½ tsp	cinnamon
2 tbsp	tomato paste
1 cup	vegetable broth
2	stalks celery, cut in 2-inch chunks
1	large carrot, halved lengthwise and cut in 1-inch chunks
4 cups	cauliflower florets
1	can (540 mL) chickpeas, drained and rinsed
½ cup	pitted prunes, halved
½ tsp	each salt and pepper
1¼ cups	whole wheat couscous
4 cups	lightly packed fresh baby spinach
1 tbsp	lemon juice
3 tbsp	slivered almonds, toasted

In Dutch oven or large heavy-bottomed saucepan, heat oil over medium heat; cook garlic and ginger, stirring, until fragrant, about 1 minute. Add onion, coriander, turmeric and cinnamon; cook, stirring often, until onion is softened, about 5 minutes. Stir in tomato paste; cook for 1 minute.

Add 1¼ cups water, the broth, celery and carrot; bring to boil. Reduce heat, cover and simmer until celery is softened, about 15 minutes. Stir in cauliflower, chickpeas, prunes, salt and pepper; bring to boil. Reduce heat, cover and simmer, stirring occasionally, until cauliflower is tender, about 15 minutes.

Meanwhile, stir couscous with 1⅓ cups boiling water. Cover and let stand for 5 minutes; fluff with fork. Stir spinach and lemon juice into cauliflower mixture; cook just until spinach is wilted. Serve over couscous; sprinkle with almonds.

NUTRITIONAL INFORMATION PER SERVING about 343 cal, 13 g pro, 6 g total fat (1 g sat. fat), 65 g carb (14 g dietary fibre, 13 g sugar), 1 mg chol, 554 mg sodium, 642 mg potassium. % RDI: 10% calcium, 29% iron, 50% vit A, 62% vit C, 51% folate.

MAKES 4 SERVINGS
HANDS-ON TIME 15 MINUTES
TOTAL TIME 15 MINUTES

Chicken Couscous Bowl

1 tsp	grated lemon zest
3 tbsp	each lemon juice and extra-virgin olive oil
¼ tsp	each ground cumin, ground ginger, salt and pepper
pinch	cinnamon
2 cups	each cooked couscous and shredded cooked chicken
1 cup	diced sweet red pepper
¼ cup	mixed olives (green and black), pitted and chopped
3 tbsp	raisins
1	green onion, sliced

In large bowl, whisk together lemon zest, lemon juice, oil, cumin, ginger, salt, pepper and cinnamon. Toss with couscous and chicken, red pepper, olives and raisins. Sprinkle with green onion.

NUTRITIONAL INFORMATION PER SERVING about 337 cal, 19 g pro, 15 g total fat (3 g sat. fat), 31 g carb (2 g dietary fibre, 7 g sugar), 46 mg chol, 305 mg sodium, 331 mg potassium. % RDI: 3% calcium, 13% iron, 12% vit A, 113% vit C, 12% folate.

MAKES 6 SERVINGS
PREP 10 MINUTES
COOK 26 MINUTES

Israeli Couscous Pilaf

2 tbsp	olive oil
¼ cup	slivered almonds
half	small onion, diced,
2 cups	Israeli couscous
1 cup	sodium-reduced chicken broth
¼ cup	dried apricots, sliced
2 tbsp	golden raisins
¼ cup	sliced green olives

In saucepan, heat oil over medium-high heat; cook almonds until golden, 1 to 2 minutes. Using slotted spoon, transfer to paper towel.

Add onion to pan; cook, stirring, until softened, about 6 minutes.

Add Israeli couscous; cook, stirring, for 1 minute. Stir in chicken broth and 1 cup water; bring to boil. Stir in apricots and golden raisins. Reduce heat to medium-low; cover and simmer until no liquid remains, about 18 minutes. Stir in olives and almonds.

NUTRITIONAL INFORMATION PER SERVING about 298 cal, 9 g pro, 8 g total fat (1 g sat. fat), 48 g carb, 3 g fibre, 0 mg chol, 197 mg sodium, 229 mg potassium. % RDI: 3% calcium, 8% iron, 2% vit A, 13% folate.

Israeli Couscous Salad
With Turkey & Honey-Roasted Carrots

MAKES 4 SERVINGS
HANDS-ON TIME 25 MINUTES
TOTAL TIME 45 MINUTES

COUSCOUS SALAD Peel carrots; cut into 1½-inch lengths. Slice lengthwise. Toss with honey, oil, salt and cumin; spread on parchment paper–lined baking sheet. Bake in 425°F oven, turning once, until golden and tender, about 30 minutes.

Meanwhile, cook couscous according to package directions; let cool slightly.

ORANGE VINAIGRETTE In large bowl, whisk together oil, orange zest, orange juice, vinegar, mustard, salt, pepper and cumin until well combined.

ASSEMBLY Add carrots, couscous, turkey, cilantro, currants and almonds to vinaigrette; toss gently to coat.

NUTRITIONAL INFORMATION PER SERVING about 520 cal, 29 g pro, 23 g total fat (4 g sat. fat), 50 g carb (4 g dietary fibre, 14 g sugar), 56 mg chol, 270 mg sodium, 687 mg potassium. % RDI: 7% calcium, 20% iron, 121% vit A, 18% vit C, 21% folate.

COUSCOUS SALAD

4	carrots
2 tsp	liquid honey
2 tsp	olive oil
pinch	each salt and ground cumin
1 cup	Israeli couscous
2 cups	shredded cooked turkey
⅓ cup	fresh cilantro leaves, torn
¼ cup	dried currants
¼ cup	toasted sliced natural (skin-on) almonds

ORANGE VINAIGRETTE

¼ cup	olive oil
½ tsp	grated orange zest
3 tbsp	orange juice
2 tbsp	white wine vinegar
1 tsp	Dijon mustard
¼ tsp	salt
pinch	each pepper and ground cumin

TIP FROM THE TEST KITCHEN

Also known as pearl couscous, Israeli couscous is much larger than the more common North African variety, making it ideal for hearty salads. Look for it in the international section of grocery stores. In many recipes, you can substitute with barley or quinoa.

H MAKES 4 TO 6 SERVINGS
ANDS-ON TIME 30 MINUTES
TOTAL TIME 40 MINUTES

Classic Risotto

½ **cup**	dry white wine
½ **tsp**	saffron threads, crumbled
3 cups	sodium-reduced chicken broth
¼ **cup**	butter
1	onion, chopped
¼ **tsp**	each salt and pepper
2 cups	arborio rice
½ **cup**	finely grated Parmesan cheese
2 tbsp	chopped fresh parsley

Stir wine with saffron; let stand for at least 10 minutes or up to 20 minutes.

In saucepan, bring broth with 3 cups water to simmer; keep warm.

In large skillet, melt 2 tbsp of the butter over medium heat; cook onion, salt and pepper, stirring occasionally, until onion is softened, about 5 minutes. Add rice, stirring.

Pour in saffron mixture; cook, stirring, until most of the liquid is absorbed, about 1 minute. Reduce heat to medium-low. Add broth mixture, ½ cup at a time, stirring after each addition until most of the liquid is absorbed before adding more, about 20 minutes total. (Rice should be loose and creamy yet still slightly firm in centre.) Stir in remaining butter, half of the cheese and the parsley. Sprinkle with remaining cheese.

NUTRITIONAL INFORMATION PER EACH OF 6 SERVINGS about 364 cal, 9 g pro, 11 g total fat (6 g sat. fat), 56 g carb, 1 g fibre, 28 mg chol, 584 mg sodium. % RDI: 10% calcium, 5% iron, 9% vit A, 3% vit C, 4% folate.

VARIATION

Arancini (Leftover Risotto Balls)

In bowl, beat 1 large egg; stir in 2 cups cold Classic Risotto and ¼ cup each dried bread crumbs and grated Parmesan cheese. Divide into 12 portions; roll into balls. Insert one ½-inch cube of mozzarella cheese into each; roll to enclose. Place on waxed paper–lined sheet; cover and refrigerate until firm, 2 hours.

Place ⅔ cup all-purpose flour in shallow dish. In separate shallow dish, add 1 large egg, lightly beaten. In third shallow dish, add ⅔ cup dried bread crumbs. One at a time, roll balls in flour. Dip into egg and then roll in crumbs to coat.

In deep-fryer or large saucepan, heat 3 cups vegetable oil until deep-fryer thermometer reads 350°F or 1-inch cube of white bread turns golden in 65 seconds. Working in batches, fry risotto balls until brown and heated through, about 4 minutes. Drain on paper towel–lined tray.

Shortcut Turkey Risotto

MAKES 4 TO 6 SERVINGS
HANDS-ON TIME 25 MINUTES
TOTAL TIME 40 MINUTES

1 tbsp	butter
1	onion, chopped
2	carrots, diced
2	cloves garlic, minced
1 tbsp	chopped fresh thyme
1½ cups	arborio rice
¼ tsp	each salt, pepper and crumbled dried sage
3 cups	sodium-reduced chicken broth
2 cups	shredded cooked turkey breast
1	zucchini, diced
1 tbsp	lemon juice
⅓ cup	finely grated Parmesan cheese

In large saucepan over medium heat, melt butter; cook onion, carrots, garlic and thyme until onion is softened, about 5 minutes. Add rice, salt, pepper and sage, stirring to coat and toast grains, about 1 minute.

Add broth and 2 cups water; bring to boil, stirring constantly. Reduce heat, cover and simmer until rice is creamy and tender, about 15 minutes. Stir in turkey and zucchini; cook, stirring, until heated through, about 2 minutes. Stir in lemon juice and half of Parmesan. Serve immediately, topped with remaining Parmesan.

NUTRITIONAL INFORMATION PER EACH OF 6 SERVINGS about 559 cal, 18 g pro, 34 g total fat (21 g sat. fat), 46 g carb (2 g dietary fibre, 3 g sugar), 110 mg chol, 733 mg sodium, 322 mg potassium. % RDI: 9% calcium, 8% iron, 73% vit A, 7% vit C, 8% folate.

TIP FROM THE TEST KITCHEN

For the best texture, serve risotto right away; as it stands, it thickens quickly and loses some of its creamy texture.

MAKES 4 TO 6 SERVINGS
HANDS-ON TIME 40 MINUTES
TOTAL TIME 2 HOURS

Beet Risotto

2	red beets
2½ cups	sodium-reduced vegetable broth
2 tbsp	butter
3	shallots, chopped
2 tsp	chopped fresh thyme
1⅓ cups	arborio rice
½ cup	dry white wine
¾ cup	finely grated Parmesan cheese
½ tsp	each salt and pepper
4 tsp	lemon juice
2 tsp	olive oil
2 cups	chopped beet greens (about 1 bunch)

Wrap each beet in foil; bake in 400°F oven until tender, about 1 hour. Let cool enough to handle. Peel and dice to make 1½ cups. *(Make-ahead: Refrigerate in airtight container for up to 48 hours.)*

While beets are cooling, in small saucepan, bring broth and 1½ cups water to boil. Reduce heat to low and keep warm.

Meanwhile, in large skillet, melt butter over medium heat; cook shallots, stirring occasionally, until softened, about 5 minutes. Add thyme; cook, stirring, until fragrant, about 30 seconds. Add rice; cook, stirring to coat and toast grains, about 1 minute. Pour in wine; cook, stirring, until most of the liquid is absorbed, about 1 minute.

Add broth mixture, ½ cup at a time, stirring after each addition until most of the liquid is absorbed before adding more, about 18 minutes total. (Rice should be loose and creamy yet still slightly firm in centre.) Stir in beets, ½ cup of the Parmesan and all but pinch each of the salt and pepper. Remove from heat. Stir in lemon juice.

While risotto is cooking, in nonstick skillet, heat oil over medium heat; cook beet greens, stirring occasionally, until wilted, about 2 minutes. Sprinkle with remaining salt and pepper. Top risotto with beet greens and remaining Parmesan.

NUTRITIONAL INFORMATION PER EACH OF 6 SERVINGS about 303 cal, 9 g pro, 9 g total fat (5 g sat. fat), 44 g carb (2 g dietary fibre, 4 g sugar), 21 mg chol, 698 mg sodium, 357 mg potassium. % RDI: 16% calcium, 9% iron, 16% vit A, 10% vit C, 19% folate.

Turkish Egg Tartines

MAKES 4 SERVINGS
HANDS-ON TIME 20 MINUTES
TOTAL TIME 30 MINUTES

YOGURT SAUCE

½ cup	grated English cucumber
½ tsp	salt
1 cup	2% Greek yogurt
2	cloves garlic, minced
2 tbsp	chopped fresh dill

PAPRIKA BUTTER

2 tbsp	unsalted butter
1½ tsp	smoked paprika
½ tsp	chili powder
¼ tsp	ground cumin

TARTINES

1 tbsp	olive oil
1 tbsp	lemon juice
½ cup	lightly packed arugula
½ cup	fresh cilantro or fresh parsley
¼ cup	fresh mint
1 tbsp	fresh dill (optional)
pinch	each salt and pepper
4	thick slices pumpernickel bread, toasted
8	soft-poached large eggs

YOGURT SAUCE Mix cucumber with salt; let stand for 10 minutes. Wrap in clean tea towel and then squeeze to remove excess liquid. In small bowl, stir together cucumber, yogurt, garlic and dill. *(Make-ahead: Cover with plastic wrap; refrigerate for up to 2 days.)*

PAPRIKA BUTTER In small microwaveable bowl, combine butter, paprika, chili powder and cumin. Microwave on medium until melted, about 45 seconds.

TARTINES In bowl, whisk oil with lemon juice. Add arugula, cilantro, mint and dill (if using); toss to coat. Sprinkle with salt and pepper. Set aside.

Spread each slice of toast with Yogurt Sauce. Top each with 2 poached eggs; drizzle with warm Paprika Butter. Top with herb mixture.

NUTRITIONAL INFORMATION PER SERVING about 534 cal, 28 g pro, 24 g total fat (9 g sat. fat), 53 g carb (8 g dietary fibre, 4 g sugar), 404 mg chol, 973 mg sodium, 542 mg potassium. % RDI: 28% calcium, 39% iron, 36% vit A, 8% vit C, 60% folate.

TIP FROM THE TEST KITCHEN

To keep poached eggs heated, place them in a bowl of warm water. Before serving, transfer briefly to a paper towel–lined plate to dry.

MAKES 6 SERVINGS
HANDS-ON TIME 40 MINUTES
TOTAL TIME 1¼ HOURS

Spanish Tortilla
With Red Pepper & Chorizo

¼ cup	extra-virgin olive oil
675 g	yellow-fleshed potatoes, peeled, halved and sliced ⅛ inch thick
2	onions, finely chopped
½ tsp	salt
¼ tsp	pepper
2	cloves garlic, minced
1	small sweet red pepper, diced
170 g	hot Spanish chorizo sausages, thinly sliced
6	large eggs
2	green onions, thinly sliced

In 12-inch nonstick ovenproof skillet, heat oil over medium-high heat; cook potatoes, onions, ¼ tsp of the salt and the pepper for 2 minutes, turning to coat.

Add garlic; cover and cook over medium heat, turning potatoes occasionally, until golden and tender, 12 to 15 minutes. Remove from pan; drain and reserve oil.

Add red pepper and chorizo to pan; cook, stirring often, until pepper is tender-crisp, 3 to 5 minutes. Add to potato mixture.

In large bowl, beat together eggs, green onions and remaining salt; stir in potato mixture.

Wipe out skillet. Add 1 tbsp of the reserved oil and heat over medium-high heat. Pour in egg mixture and cook until edge starts to set, 1 to 2 minutes.

Transfer skillet to 350°F oven. Bake until knife inserted in centre comes out clean, 20 to 25 minutes. Let stand for 5 minutes before cutting.

NUTRITIONAL INFORMATION PER SERVING about 358 cal, 15 g pro, 23 g total fat (7 g sat. fat), 23 g carb (2 g dietary fibre), 211 mg chol, 608 mg sodium, 593 mg potassium. % RDI: 4% calcium, 11% iron, 12% vit A, 53% vit C, 20% folate.

TIP FROM THE TEST KITCHEN

For a tapas-style meal, serve this Spanish Tortilla and Spanish Salt Cod Fritters (see recipe, page 18) with small dishes of marinated olives, slices of Manchego cheese, and garlic prawns.

To make garlic prawns, combine chopped garlic, red pepper flakes and olive oil in a small baking dish, and bake in 450°F oven until the mixture sizzles. Add peeled and deveined shrimp and bake until cooked through, about 10 minutes. Serve with crusty bread to sop up the spicy garlic oil.

Walnut Pesto Frittata
With Prosciutto & Mozzarella

MAKES 4 TO 6 SERVINGS
HANDS-ON TIME 20 MINUTES
TOTAL TIME 40 MINUTES

WALNUT PESTO

¼ cup	chopped walnuts, toasted
1	clove garlic
1¼ cups	fresh basil leaves
¼ cup	finely grated Parmesan cheese
pinch	each salt and pepper
5 tbsp	olive oil

FRITTATA

4 tsp	vegetable oil
1	onion, sliced
12	large eggs
¼ cup	milk
¼ tsp	each salt and pepper
100 g	fresh mozzarella cheese, sliced
45 g	thinly sliced prosciutto

WALNUT PESTO In food processor, pulse walnuts with garlic until coarsely ground. Add basil, Parmesan, salt and pepper; pulse until combined. With motor running, add oil in thin steady stream until smooth. Reserve half of the pesto; refrigerate remainder for another use. *(Make-ahead: Refrigerate in airtight container for up to 3 days or freeze for up to 6 months.)*

FRITTATA In 10-inch ovenproof nonstick or cast-iron skillet, heat oil over medium heat; cook onion, stirring occasionally, until softened and light golden, about 12 minutes.

Meanwhile, beat together eggs, milk, salt and pepper. Pour over onion mixture in pan; reduce heat to medium-low and cook until bottom and sides are set but top is still slightly runny, about 15 minutes.

Top with mozzarella; dot with teaspoonfuls of the reserved pesto. Broil until top is golden and set, 3 to 5 minutes. Arrange prosciutto over top; cut into wedges.

NUTRITIONAL INFORMATION PER EACH OF 6 SERVINGS about 416 cal, 15 g pro, 22 g total fat (5 g sat. fat), 4 g carb (trace dietary fibre, 2 g sugar), 375 mg chol, 434 mg sodium, 235 mg potassium. % RDI: 9% calcium, 13% iron, 22% vit A, 3% vit C, 27% folate.

TIP FROM THE TEST KITCHEN

Toss the leftover pesto with freshly cooked pasta and sprinkle with torn fresh basil for a weeknight meal that's ready in minutes.

MAKES 4 TO 6 SERVINGS
HANDS-ON TIME 10 MINUTES
TOTAL TIME 25 MINUTES

Herbed Potato Frittata

¼ cup	chopped fresh basil
3 tbsp	each chopped fresh chives and fresh dill
1 tbsp	extra-virgin olive oil
1½ cups	diced peeled cooked red or white waxy potato (about 1 large)
½ tsp	each salt and pepper
2	cloves garlic, minced
10	large eggs
170 g	smoked salmon
2 tbsp	sour cream

Stir together basil, chives and dill; set aside.

In 10-inch ovenproof or cast-iron skillet, heat oil over medium heat, brushing up side of pan. Cook potato with a pinch each of the salt and pepper, stirring, until light golden, about 5 minutes. Add garlic; cook, stirring, until fragrant, about 1 minute.

Meanwhile, in bowl, beat eggs; stir in remaining salt and pepper and all but 1 tbsp of the basil mixture. Pour over potato mixture; reduce heat to medium-low and cook until bottom and side are set but top is still slightly runny, about 15 minutes.

Broil until top is golden and set, about 2 minutes. Top with smoked salmon and sour cream. Sprinkle with remaining basil mixture.

NUTRITIONAL INFORMATION PER EACH OF 6 SERVINGS about 214 cal, 16 g pro, 12 g total fat (4 g sat. fat), 8 g carb (1 g dietary fibre, 1 g sugar), 313 mg chol, 524 mg sodium, 287 mg potassium. % RDI: 5% calcium, 12% iron, 17% vit A, 7% vit C, 24% folate.

TIP FROM THE TEST KITCHEN

If you don't have any leftover cooked potato, pierce 1 potato, scrubbed, with fork; microwave on high, turning once, until tender, about 6 minutes. Let cool; peel and dice.

Eggs Poached in Tomato Fennel Sauce

MAKES 4 SERVINGS
HANDS-ON TIME 20 MINUTES
TOTAL TIME 30 MINUTES

2 tsp	olive oil
1	small bulb fennel, trimmed, cored and thinly sliced
2	green onions, sliced (white and light green parts separated)
2 cups	plain tomato sauce
1 tsp	sherry vinegar or red wine vinegar
½ tsp	granulated sugar
4	large eggs
pinch	each salt and pepper

In large skillet, heat oil over medium heat; cook fennel and ½ cup water, stirring occasionally, until fennel is softened and water has evaporated, about 15 minutes. Add white parts of green onions; cook, stirring, until softened, about 1 minute. Stir in tomato sauce, vinegar and sugar. Bring to boil; reduce heat to simmer.

Using back of spoon, make 4 wells in sauce; gently break 1 egg into each. Sprinkle with salt and pepper. Simmer, partially covered, until egg whites are set yet yolks are still slightly runny, about 9 minutes. Sprinkle with green parts of green onions.

NUTRITIONAL INFORMATION PER SERVING about 201 cal, 9 g pro, 13 g total fat (3 g sat. fat), 14 g carb (4 g dietary fibre, 9 g sugar), 193 mg chol, 247 mg sodium, 775 mg potassium. % RDI: 7% calcium, 14% iron, 24% vit A, 45% vit C, 28% folate.

TIP FROM THE TEST KITCHEN

To avoid getting any bits of shell in the tomato mixture, crack each egg into a small bowl before tipping it into a well.

MAKES 4 SERVINGS
HANDS-ON TIME 30 MINUTES
TOTAL TIME 30 MINUTES

Tuscan Green Bean & Tuna Salad

DRESSING

½ cup	olive oil
¼ cup	white vinegar
6	anchovy fillets or 1 tbsp anchovy paste
1 tsp	liquid honey
½ tsp	pepper
¼ tsp	salt

SALAD

450 g	green beans, trimmed
1	can (540 mL) no-salt-added cannellini or white kidney beans, drained and rinsed
2 cups	croutons
¼ cup	chopped fresh dill
10	leaves radicchio, torn in bite-size pieces
160 g	oil-packed solid light albacore tuna, drained and broken in chunks
½ tsp	lemon zest
¼ cup	shaved Parmesan cheese (optional)
¼ tsp	pepper (optional)
	dill sprigs (optional)

DRESSING In liquid measure, combine oil, vinegar, anchovies, honey, pepper and salt. Using immersion blender, purée until smooth.

SALAD In large saucepan of boiling salted water, cook green beans until tender-crisp, about 2 minutes. Drain; transfer to bowl of ice water to chill. Drain well; pat dry with towel. *(Make-ahead: Refrigerate in airtight container for up to 24 hours.)*

In large bowl, combine green beans, cannellini beans, croutons, chopped dill and radicchio; drizzle with dressing, tossing to coat. Arrange salad on platter. Top with tuna and lemon zest. Garnish with Parmesan, pepper and dill sprigs (if using).

NUTRITIONAL INFORMATION PER SERVING about 499 cal, 21 g pro, 32 g total fat (5 g sat. fat), 35 g carb (11 g dietary fibre, 4 g sugar), 11 mg chol, 602 mg sodium, 663 mg potassium. % RDI: 11% calcium, 24% iron, 8% vit A, 18% vit C, 44% folate.

TIP FROM THE TEST KITCHEN

Good-quality oil-packed tuna is worth the splurge, especially in this salad. It has more moisture and flavour than water-packed.

Panzanella
With Asparagus & Eggs

MAKES 4 SERVINGS
HANDS-ON TIME 15 MINUTES
TOTAL TIME 15 MINUTES

DIJON DRESSING

2 tbsp	extra-virgin olive oil
1 tbsp	red wine vinegar
1 tsp	Dijon mustard
¼ tsp	each salt and pepper

PANZANELLA

4	large eggs (shell-on)
pinch	each salt and pepper
2	slices (½ inch thick) sourdough bread
1 tsp	extra-virgin olive oil
1	bunch asparagus (about 450 g), trimmed
1	clove garlic, halved lengthwise
1	avocado, sliced
1 cup	halved cherry tomatoes
½ cup	thinly sliced red onion
⅓ cup	torn fresh basil

DIJON DRESSING In small bowl, whisk together oil, vinegar, mustard, salt and pepper. Set aside.

PANZANELLA In saucepan, add eggs and enough water to cover by at least 1 inch; bring to boil. Reduce heat; boil gently for 4 minutes. Remove from heat and let stand for 4 minutes. Drain and run eggs under cold water for 2 minutes; drain. *(Make-ahead: Refrigerate for up to 2 days.)* Peel eggs and halve lengthwise; sprinkle with salt and pepper. Set aside.

Brush both sides of bread with oil. Place bread and asparagus on greased grill over medium-high heat; close lid and grill, turning once, until asparagus is tender and slightly grill-marked and bread is grill-marked, about 7 minutes. Rub both sides of bread with cut sides of garlic; discard garlic. Let cool slightly; cube bread and halve asparagus crosswise.

In large bowl, gently toss together bread, asparagus, avocado, tomatoes, red onion and basil.

Toss bread mixture with dressing to coat. Top with eggs.

NUTRITIONAL INFORMATION PER SERVING about 330 cal, 13 g pro, 20 g total fat (4 g sat. fat), 27 g carb (6 g dietary fibre, 4 g sugar), 216 mg chol, 443 mg sodium, 556 mg potassium. % RDI: 7% calcium, 21% iron, 20% vit A, 25% vit C, 88% folate.

MAKES 6 TO 8 SERVINGS
HANDS-ON TIME 5 MINUTES
TOTAL TIME 55 MINUTES

Grilled Eggplant Salad

2	eggplants (about 1 kg total)
4	green onions, thinly sliced
¼ cup	each chopped fresh parsley and fresh cilantro
2	cloves garlic, minced
¼ cup	extra-virgin olive oil
2 tbsp	lemon juice
¾ tsp	salt
¼ tsp	pepper
⅓ cup	walnut halves, toasted

Prick eggplants all over. Place on greased grill over medium-low heat; close lid and grill, turning often, until softened and charred, about 50 minutes. (Or place on baking sheet; bake in 350°F oven until soft, about 50 minutes.) Let cool on plate.

Peel and discard skin and any juices; chop coarsely and transfer to serving bowl. Stir in green onions, parsley, cilantro, garlic, oil, lemon juice, salt and pepper. *(Make-ahead: Cover and refrigerate for up to 8 hours.)*

Chop walnuts coarsely; sprinkle over eggplant mixture.

NUTRITIONAL INFORMATION PER EACH OF 8 SERVINGS about 129 cal, 2 g pro, 11 g total fat (2 g sat. fat), 10 g carb, 4.g dietary fibre, 0 mg chol, 224 mg sodium. % RDI: 4% iron, 11% vit A, 16% vit C, 8% folate.

MAKES 8 SERVINGS
HANDS-ON TIME 5 MINUTES
TOTAL TIME 5 MINUTES

Tomato-Feta Platter

4 to 8	small tomatoes
12	sun-dried black olives
quarter	English cucumber, thinly sliced
350 g	feta cheese, crumbled
¼ cup	extra-virgin olive oil
1 tbsp	chopped fresh parsley
½ tsp	sea salt (optional)

Core tomatoes. Cut each into 8 wedges from stem end almost to base, leaving base intact so wedges form flower shape. Arrange on serving platter.

Place 1 olive in centre of each tomato. Surround tomatoes with cucumber, feta and remaining olives. Drizzle with oil; sprinkle parsley and salt (if using) over top.

NUTRITIONAL INFORMATION PER SERVING about 194 cal, 7 g pro, 17 g total fat (8 g sat. fat), 5 g carb, 1 g dietary fibre, 39 mg chol, 553 mg sodium. % RDI: 21% calcium, 6% iron, 9% vit A, 17% vit C, 10% folate.

Arugula & Fennel Salad
With Crispy Prosciutto-Wrapped Figs

MAKES 4 SERVINGS
HANDS-ON TIME 15 MINUTES
TOTAL TIME 15 MINUTES

BALSAMIC DRESSING

8 tsp	extra-virgin olive oil
4 tsp	balsamic vinegar
1 tsp	liquid honey
¼ tsp	each salt and pepper

ARUGULA & FENNEL SALAD

6	strips prosciutto
8	small fresh Mission figs, halved lengthwise
4 cups	lightly packed baby arugula
2 cup	thinly sliced cored trimmed fennel
30 g	Parmesan cheese, shaved

BALSAMIC DRESSING In small bowl, whisk together oil, vinegar, honey, salt and pepper. *(Make-ahead: Refrigerate in airtight container for up to 3 days; shake or whisk before using.)*

ARUGULA & FENNEL SALAD Slice prosciutto lengthwise into 1-inch wide strips. Wrap 1 strip around each fig half. *(Make-ahead: Cover and refrigerate for up to 24 hours.)*

Brush figs with 2 tsp of the dressing. Place, cut side up, on greased foil-lined rimmed baking sheet. Broil until prosciutto is crisp and golden, 2 to 3 minutes.

In bowl, toss together arugula, fennel and remaining dressing. Top with figs and Parmesan.

NUTRITIONAL INFORMATION PER SERVING about 203 cal, 9 g pro, 12 g total fat (3 g sat. fat), 16 g carb (3 g dietary fibre, 8 g sugar), 25 mg chol, 638 mg sodium, 501 mg potassium. % RDI: 15% calcium, 9% iron, 7% vit A, 15% vit C, 15% folate.

TIP FROM THE TEST KITCHEN

Small figs work best in this recipe, but you can use 4 large ones, cut into quarters.

MAKES 12 SERVINGS
HANDS-ON TIME 15 MINUTES
TOTAL TIME 15 MINUTES

Blood Orange & Fennel Salad

3	small blood oranges or Cara Cara navel oranges
3 tbsp	red wine vinegar
1 tbsp	Dijon mustard
2 tsp	liquid honey
1	clove garlic, pressed or finely grated
¼ tsp	each salt and pepper
½ cup	extra-virgin olive oil
12 cups	torn red or green leaf lettuce
1	small bulb fennel, trimmed, cored and thinly sliced
¾ cup	thinly sliced red onion

Finely grate orange zest to make 1 tsp. Remove remaining peel and pith from oranges; cut oranges crosswise into generous ¼-inch thick slices. Set aside.

In small bowl, whisk together vinegar, mustard, honey, orange zest, garlic, salt and pepper. Gradually whisk in oil in thin steady stream until well combined. *(Make-ahead: Refrigerate in airtight container for up to 5 days.)*

In large bowl, combine lettuce, fennel, red onion and oranges. Drizzle with vinaigrette; toss to coat. Serve immediately.

NUTRITIONAL INFORMATION PER SERVING about 113 cal, 1 g pro, 9 g total fat (1 g sat. fat), 7 g carb (2 g dietary fibre, 5 g sugar), 0 mg chol, 82 mg sodium, 195 mg potassium. % RDI: 3% calcium, 4% iron, 35% vit A, 37% vit C, 12% folate.

TIP FROM THE TEST KITCHEN

Choose blood oranges that feel heavy for their size. Store them in your refrigerator or in a cool, dry place for up to a week. Blood oranges are in season during the winter months; Cara Cara navel oranges have a longer season.

Heirloom Tomato Tabbouleh Salad

MAKES 8 SERVINGS
HANDS-ON TIME 30 MINUTES
TOTAL TIME 30 MINUTES

¾ cup	whole grain coarse bulgur
¼ cup	red quinoa, rinsed
4	large heirloom tomatoes, cut in wedges or sliced
1	shallot, thinly sliced
1 tsp	salt
¼ cup	olive oil
2 tbsp	lemon juice
2 tbsp	pomegranate molasses or balsamic glaze
½ cup	coarsely chopped fresh parsley
½ cup	coarsely chopped fresh mint
quarter	English cucumber, thinly sliced
¼ cup	pine nuts, toasted

In saucepan, bring 2 cups water to boil. Stir in bulgur and quinoa; return to boil. Reduce heat to low and simmer, covered, until no liquid remains, 15 to 18 minutes. Fluff with fork; let cool.

Meanwhile, in large bowl, gently toss together tomatoes, shallot and ½ tsp of the salt. Let stand.

In small bowl, whisk together oil, lemon juice, molasses and remaining salt. Pour over bulgur mixture. Add parsley, mint and cucumber; toss to mix. Spoon onto platter; top with tomato mixture. Sprinkle with pine nuts. *(Make-ahead: Stir together bulgur, quinoa and dressing; refrigerate in airtight container for up to 24 hours. Just before serving, toss with tomatoes, shallot, parsley, mint and cucumber; sprinkle with pine nuts.)*

NUTRITIONAL INFORMATION PER SERVING about 203 cal, 5 g pro, 10 g total fat (1 g sat. fat), 25 g carb (5 g dietary fibre, 6 g sugar), 0 mg chol, 300 mg sodium, 438 mg potassium. % RDI: 4% calcium, 17% iron, 15% vit A, 33% vit C, 17% folate.

TIP FROM THE TEST KITCHEN

For a gluten-free version of this salad, omit the bulgur and use 1 cup red quinoa. If you use balsamic vinegar, check the label: Some brands may contain gluten.

MAKES 4 SERVINGS
HANDS-ON TIME 15 MINUTES
TOTAL TIME 15 MINUTES

Halloumi Salad With Herbed Pita Chips

HERBED PITA CHIPS

1	Greek pita
1 tsp	olive oil
¼ tsp	each dried basil and dried oregano

SALAD

half	pkg (250 g pkg) halloumi cheese, cut crosswise in scant ¼-inch thick slices
2 tbsp	extra-virgin olive oil
1 tbsp	red wine vinegar
1	clove garlic, minced
¼ tsp	dried oregano
pinch	pepper
5 cups	mixed baby greens
1	sweet green pepper, chopped
1	pkg (250 g) cherry tomatoes or grape tomatoes, halved
half	English cucumber, chopped
half	red onion, thinly sliced
½ cup	pitted Kalamata olives

HERBED PITA CHIPS Brush pita with oil; sprinkle with basil and oregano. Cut into 8 wedges; arrange in single layer on rimmed baking sheet. Bake in 350°F oven until crisp and light golden, about 8 minutes. *(Make-ahead: Let cool completely; store in airtight container for up to 2 days.)*

SALAD While pita is baking, in nonstick skillet, cook halloumi over medium heat, turning once, until light golden, about 3 minutes.

Meanwhile, in large bowl, whisk together oil, vinegar, garlic, oregano and pepper. Add baby greens, green pepper, tomatoes, cucumber, red onion and olives; toss to coat. Divide among 4 serving plates; top with halloumi. Serve with pita chips.

NUTRITIONAL INFORMATION PER SERVING about 296 cal, 10 g pro, 21 g total fat (7 g sat. fat), 19 g carb (3 g dietary fibre, 5 g sugar), 31 mg chol, 743 mg sodium, 453 mg potassium. % RDI: 21% calcium, 11% iron, 42% vit A, 82% vit C, 24% folate.

TIP FROM THE TEST KITCHEN

To pit olives quickly, spread them onto a cutting board and press with the bottom of a saucepan. This exposes the pits, making them easy to remove.

Roasted Cauliflower
With Lemon-Garlic Tahini

MAKES 6 SERVINGS
HANDS-ON TIME 25 MINUTES
TOTAL TIME 1½ HOURS

LEMON-GARLIC TAHINI

half	head garlic
1 tsp	olive oil
⅓ cup	tahini
⅓ cup	lemon juice
1 tbsp	liquid honey
1 tsp	salt
½ tsp	ground cumin
½ tsp	ground sumac
3 tbsp	chopped fresh parsley or fresh cilantro

ROASTED CAULIFLOWER

16 cups	bite-size cauliflower florets (about 1 large head)
¼ cup	olive oil
3 tbsp	chopped fresh thyme
1 tbsp	coriander seeds, lightly crushed
1 tbsp	fennel seeds, lightly crushed
1 tsp	ground sumac
⅓ cup	pomegranate seeds
3 tbsp	chopped fresh parsley or fresh cilantro

LEMON-GARLIC TAHINI Slice top third off half garlic head to expose cloves; discard. Drizzle cloves with oil; wrap in foil. Bake in 400°F oven until tender, about 30 minutes; let cool slightly. Squeeze cloves into blender.

In blender, purée together garlic, 6 tbsp water, tahini, lemon juice, honey, salt, cumin and sumac. Add parsley; blend until combined. *(Make-ahead: Refrigerate in airtight container for up to 1 week.)*

ROASTED CAULIFLOWER In large bowl, toss together cauliflower, oil, thyme, coriander seeds, fennel seeds and sumac. Arrange in single layer on 2 parchment paper–lined rimmed baking sheets. Bake in 425°F oven, turning once, until tender and golden brown, 35 to 40 minutes. Scrape into same bowl; toss with lemon-garlic tahini and half each of the pomegranate seeds and parsley. Transfer to large platter; sprinkle with remaining pomegranate seeds and parsley.

NUTRITIONAL INFORMATION PER SERVING about 246 cal, 7 g pro, 18 g total fat (3 g sat. fat), 19 g carb (8 g dietary fibre, 7 g sugar), 0 mg chol, 458 mg sodium, 436 mg potassium. % RDI: 11% calcium, 21% iron, 4% vit A, 165% vit C, 49% folate.

MAKES 4 SERVINGS
HANDS-ON TIME 5 MINUTES
TOTAL TIME 30 MINUTES

Braised Artichokes
With Spiced Feta & Mint

2	lemons
3 tbsp	olive oil
2	cloves garlic, thinly sliced
4	large artichokes, trimmed and halved lengthwise
1 tsp	salt
60 g	feta cheese, crumbled
1 tsp	Asian chili sauce (such as sriracha)
2 tbsp	chopped fresh mint

Halve and juice lemons, reserving lemon halves. Set aside.

In skillet, heat 2 tbsp of the oil over medium heat; cook garlic, stirring, until golden, about 1 minute. Add lemon juice, reserved lemon halves, artichokes, salt and 4 cups water; bring to boil. Reduce heat, cover and simmer until artichokes are fork-tender, about 20 minutes. Drain. Let cool enough to handle.

Using teaspoon, remove choke from centre of each artichoke; discard. Arrange artichokes, cut side up, in 8-inch square baking dish. Discard lemon halves.

Mix feta with chili sauce; sprinkle over artichokes. Broil until feta is golden, about 3 minutes. Sprinkle with mint. Drizzle with remaining oil.

NUTRITIONAL INFORMATION PER SERVING about 133 cal, 6 g pro, 7 g total fat (3 g sat. fat), 15 g carb (11 g dietary fibre, 2 g sugar), 14 mg chol, 538 mg sodium, 366 mg potassium. % RDI: 10% calcium, 9% iron, 3% vit A, 15% vit C, 52% folate.

TIP FROM THE TEST KITCHEN

To trim and prepare an artichoke for cooking, slice off the top third, and peel off the thick outer leaves (called bracts). Using a vegetable peeler, remove the outer layer of the base and the stem. Cut artichokes brown quickly when exposed to air; keep a lemon half handy to rub on any exposed surfaces. As you trim each artichoke, place it in a bowl of ice water and a squeeze of lemon juice.

Many recipes call for slicing trimmed artichokes in half lengthwise before cooking; this exposes the fuzzy choke, making it easy to remove later.

Cheesy Polenta Squares

MAKES 10 TO 12 SERVINGS
HANDS-ON TIME 20 MINUTES
TOTAL TIME 1½ HOURS

2 tbsp	butter
2 tsp	each dried thyme and dried sage
¼ tsp	each garlic powder, salt and pepper
pinch	nutmeg
2 cups	sodium-reduced chicken broth
1 cup	cornmeal
⅓ cup	finely grated Parmesan cheese
¼ cup	shredded Gruyère cheese
¼ cup	sour cream
1 tbsp	each Dijon mustard and lemon juice
2 tbsp	olive oil
2 tbsp	chopped fresh parsley or fresh chives

In saucepan, melt butter over medium heat; cook thyme, sage, garlic powder, salt, pepper and nutmeg, stirring, until fragrant, about 1 minute. Stir in broth and ⅓ cup water; bring to boil. Reduce heat to medium and gradually whisk in cornmeal; cook, stirring often, until thick enough to mound on spoon, about 5 minutes. Stir in Parmesan and Gruyère until melted, about 30 seconds. Remove from heat; stir in sour cream, mustard and lemon juice.

Scrape polenta into parchment paper–lined 9-inch square cake pan, smoothing top. Let cool slightly, about 15 minutes. Refrigerate until firm, about 1 hour. *(Make-ahead: Refrigerate for up to 48 hours.)* Cut into generous 1-inch squares.

In large skillet, heat half of the oil over medium-high heat; cook half of the polenta, gently turning occasionally, until golden, about 5 minutes. Transfer to serving platter. Repeat with remaining oil and polenta. Sprinkle with parsley.

NUTRITIONAL INFORMATION PER EACH OF 12 SERVINGS about 121 cal, 4 g pro, 7 g total fat (3 g sat. fat), 12 g carb (1 g dietary fibre, trace sugar), 12 mg chol, 234 mg sodium, 45 mg potassium. % RDI: 6% calcium, 4% iron, 4% vit A, 2% vit C, 3% folate.

MAKES 8 SERVINGS
HANDS-ON TIME 25 MINUTES
TOTAL TIME 1¾ HOURS

Herbed Potato Gnocchi

1.25 kg	yellow-fleshed potatoes (about 6)
1	egg yolk
¼ cup	finely chopped fresh parsley
2 tbsp	minced fresh herbs (such as thyme, sage or rosemary)
1 tsp	salt
2⅓ cups	all-purpose flour
¼ cup	butter

In large saucepan of boiling salted water, cover and cook potatoes until tender, about 30 minutes. Drain and let cool enough to handle, about 10 minutes. Peel and place in large bowl; refrigerate until cold, about 30 minutes.

Using medium disc of food mill or ricer or with potato masher, press potatoes into bowl. Using fork, mix in egg yolk, parsley, minced herbs and salt. Using wooden spoon, mix in 2 cups of the flour, 1 cup at a time. Turn out onto unfloured work surface. Knead to form soft, slightly sticky, spongy dough.

Divide dough into 8 pieces. Roll out each into 20-inch rope about ¾ inch thick; cut each into ½-inch lengths. On work surface, toss with remaining flour; transfer to lightly floured waxed paper–lined baking sheet. *(Make-ahead: Freeze for 2 hours or until firm; using metal spatula, scrape into freezer bags and freeze for up to 2 weeks.)*

Fill large bowl with ice water. In large saucepan of boiling salted water, cook gnocchi, in 3 batches, just until tender, about 3 minutes. Using slotted spoon, transfer to ice water and stir until cold; transfer to towel-lined tray; arrange in single layer and pat dry. *(Make-ahead: Cover with plastic wrap and refrigerate for up to 24 hours.)*

In large nonstick skillet, heat half of the butter over medium-heat; cook gnocchi, in 3 batches, stirring occasionally and adding remaining butter as necessary, until golden, about 5 minutes.

NUTRITIONAL INFORMATION PER SERVING about 286 cal, 6 g pro, 7 g total fat (4 g sat. fat), 50 g carb, 44 mg chol, 755 mg sodium. % RDI: 2% calcium, 16% iron, 8% vit A, 27% vit C, 28% folate.

Ricotta Gnocchi With Sautéed Beets

MAKES 4 SERVINGS
HANDS-ON TIME 30 MINUTES
TOTAL TIME 30 MINUTES

RICOTTA GNOCCHI In bowl, stir together ricotta, flour, eggs, Parmesan and salt to make ragged dough. Turn out onto lightly floured surface; divide into quarters. Working with one quarter at a time, with floured hands, roll dough into ¾-inch thick rope; cut crosswise into ¾-inch long pieces. Set aside on floured waxed paper–lined baking sheet.

In large saucepan of boiling salted water, cook gnocchi, in batches, until floating and no longer doughy in centre, about 3 minutes. Using slotted spoon, transfer to plate. Set aside; keep warm.

SAUTÉED BEETS In large skillet, heat oil over medium heat; cook garlic, stirring, until fragrant and light golden, about 1 minute. Stir in beets; cook, stirring occasionally, until tender-crisp, about 8 minutes. Stir in beet greens, gnocchi, walnuts and salt; cook, stirring occasionally, until greens are wilted and gnocchi are warmed through, about 2 minutes.

NUTRITIONAL INFORMATION PER SERVING about 687 cal, 30 g pro, 40 g total fat (15 g sat. fat), 54 g carb (5 g dietary fibre, 11 g sugar), 132 mg chol, 1,035 mg sodium, 628 mg potassium. % RDI: 34% calcium, 36% iron, 42% vit A, 12% vit C, 80% folate.

RICOTTA GNOCCHI

- **1** tub (475 g) extra-smooth ricotta cheese
- **1¾ cups** all-purpose flour
- **2** eggs, beaten
- **½ cup** finely shredded Parmesan cheese
- **¼ tsp** salt

SAUTÉED BEETS

- **2 tbsp** olive oil
- **2** cloves garlic, thinly sliced
- **6** baby golden beets (about 2 inches diameter), peeled, halved and thinly sliced
- **2 cups** lightly packed chopped beet greens
- **⅔ cup** chopped walnuts, toasted
- **pinch** salt

TIP FROM THE TEST KITCHEN

If your beets don't have the greens attached, substitute an equal amount of chopped Swiss chard leaves. And if you can't find baby golden beets, substitute about three 3½-inch golden beets and cut them into wedges before slicing thinly.

MAKES 4 TO 6 SERVINGS
HANDS-ON TIME 5 MINUTES
TOTAL TIME 3¼ HOURS

Slow Cooker Moroccan Carrots

12	small carrots (about 1 kg total)
1	onion
3	cloves garlic, sliced
⅓ cup	chicken or vegetable broth
2 tbsp	butter
½ tsp	salt
¼ tsp	ground cumin
pinch	cayenne pepper (optional)
1 tbsp	cornstarch
1 tbsp	minced fresh cilantro or fresh parsley

Peel carrots and cut into 2-inch long pencil-thin sticks. Peel and halve onion; slice crosswise.

Add carrots, onion, garlic, broth, butter, salt, cumin, and cayenne (if using) to slow cooker; stir to coat carrots. Cover and cook on low until carrots are tender, about 3 hours.

Whisk cornstarch with 2 tbsp water; drizzle over carrots. Toss to combine. Cover and cook on high until sauce becomes clear, about 10 minutes. Sprinkle with cilantro.

NUTRITIONAL INFORMATION PER EACH OF 6 SERVINGS about 93 cal, 1 g pro, 4 g total fat (3 g sat. fat), 14 g carb, 4 g dietary fibre, 10 mg chol, 341 mg sodium. % RDI: 4% calcium, 4% iron, 212% vit A, 8% vit C, 9% folate.

MAKES 4 SERVINGS
HANDS-ON TIME 8 MINUTES
TOTAL TIME 20 MINUTES

Roasted Asparagus
With Lemon & Parmesan

On baking sheet, sprinkle 1 bunch (about 450 g) asparagus, trimmed, with 2 tsp olive oil, 1 tsp grated lemon zest, pinch each salt and pepper; toss to coat. Bake in 425°F oven, shaking pan halfway through, until tender-crisp, about 12 minutes.

Toss with 2 tbsp lemon juice. Arrange on serving platter; top with shaved Parmesan cheese (about 17 g).

NUTRITIONAL INFORMATION PER SERVING about 56 cal, 4 g pro, 4 g total fat (1 g sat. fat), 4 g carb (2 g dietary fibre, 1 g sugar), 3 mg chol, 79 mg sodium, 191 mg potassium. % RDI: 6% calcium, 6% iron, 8% vit A, 17% vit C, 54% folate.

Lemony Roasted Potatoes

MAKES 8 SERVINGS
HANDS-ON TIME 15 MINUTES
TOTAL TIME 1¼ HOURS

8	yellow-fleshed potatoes scrubbed (about 2 kg total)
½ cup	lemon juice
⅓ cup	extra-virgin olive oil
3	cloves garlic, minced
2 tsp	salt
2 tsp	dried oregano
1 tsp	pepper

In large saucepan of boiling salted water, cover and cook potatoes until slightly tender, about 15 minutes. Drain and let cool. Peel; cut into wedges.

In large bowl, whisk together lemon juice, oil, garlic, salt, oregano and pepper; add potatoes and toss gently to coat. (*Make-ahead: Cover and refrigerate for up to 4 hours.*)

Arrange potatoes on parchment paper–lined or greased rimmed baking sheet. Roast in 400°F oven, turning once, until tender-crisp and most liquid is evaporated, about 40 minutes.

NUTRITIONAL INFORMATION PER SERVING about 247 cal, 4 g pro, 9 g total fat (1 g sat. fat), 39 g carb, 0 mg chol, 1,030 mg sodium. % RDI: 2% calcium, 13% iron, 43% vit C, 10% folate.

Sicilian-Style Kale With Golden Raisins

MAKES 8 SERVINGS
HANDS-ON TIME 8 MINUTES
TOTAL TIME 20 MINUTES

In large skillet, heat 4 tsp olive oil over medium-high heat. Add 2 large bunches kale, stemmed and chopped; ½ cup golden raisins; ¼ tsp each salt and pepper; and ½ cup water. Cook, stirring, until kale is slightly softened and water has evaporated, about 6 minutes. Arrange on serving platter; sprinkle with 2 tbsp toasted sliced almonds.

NUTRITIONAL INFORMATION PER SERVING about 72 cal, 2 g pro, 4 g total fat (0.3 g sat. fat), 11 g carb (2 g dietary fibre, 6 g sugar), 0 mg chol, 85 mg sodium, 196 mg potassium. % RDI: 5% calcium, 4% iron, 136% vit A, 35% vit C, 2% folate.

MAKES 8 TO 10 SERVINGS
HANDS-ON TIME 20 MINUTES
TOTAL TIME 20 MINUTES

Cremini Mushrooms & Asparagus
With Pancetta

1	pkg (150 g) diced pancetta
3	shallots, sliced
3	bunches (each 450 g) asparagus, trimmed and cut in 2½-inch pieces
2	pkg (each 227 g) cremini mushrooms, quartered
½ tsp	pepper
pinch	salt
2 tbsp	red wine vinegar

In large nonstick skillet over medium-high heat, cook pancetta, stirring occasionally, until crisp, about 5 minutes.

Add shallots, asparagus, mushrooms, pepper and salt; cook, stirring occasionally, until asparagus is tender-crisp, about 8 minutes. Stir in vinegar.

NUTRITIONAL INFORMATION PER EACH OF 10 SERVINGS about 79 cal, 7 g pro, 4 g total fat (1 g sat. fat), 6 g carb (3 g dietary fibre, 2 g sugar), 14 mg chol, 212 mg sodium, 426 mg potassium. % RDI: 3% calcium, 9% iron, 10% vit A, 12% vit C, 66% folate.

MAKES 4 SERVINGS
HANDS-ON TIME 15 MINUTES
TOTAL TIME 15 MINUTES

Mushroom-Tomato Medley

In skillet, heat 1 tbsp vegetable oil over medium heat. Add 1 onion, chopped; 1 garlic clove, minced; 3 cups quartered button mushrooms (about 250 g); and ¼ tsp each salt and pepper. Cook, stirring often, until onions are softened, about 5 minutes.

Sprinkle with 1 tbsp all-purpose flour; cook, stirring, for 1 minute. Stir in ½ cup chicken broth and bring to boil; reduce heat and simmer for 2 minutes. Add 2 cups cherry tomatoes, halved; cook until some juice is released, about 3 minutes.

NUTRITIONAL INFORMATION PER SERVING about 75 cal, 3 g pro, 4 g total fat (trace sat. fat), 9 g carb, 0 mg chol, 247 mg sodium. % RDI: 1% calcium, 9% iron, 7% vit A, 20% vit C, 7% folate.

Cremini Mushrooms & Asparagus With Pancetta

Pear & Walnut Baklava

MAKES 18 PIECES
HANDS-ON TIME 30 MINUTES
TOTAL TIME 2½ HOURS

2 cups	diced cored peeled Bosc pears (about 2)
⅔ cup	fresh or frozen cranberries
3 tbsp	cornstarch
½ tsp	each ground cinnamon and ground ginger
¼ tsp	nutmeg
6	sheets frozen phyllo pastry, thawed
¼ cup	butter, melted
¾ cup	finely chopped walnuts (about 115 g)
¾ cup	granulated sugar
1	piece (1½ inches) fresh ginger, peeled and thinly sliced
2	cinnamon sticks
5	whole cloves
4	strips (1 inch wide) orange zest
1 tsp	lemon juice

In bowl, toss together pears, cranberries, cornstarch, ground cinnamon, ground ginger and nutmeg to coat.

Halve phyllo sheets crosswise; trim to fit 9-inch square cake pan. Keeping remainder covered with damp towel (to prevent drying out), place 1 halved phyllo sheet in bottom of pan; brush lightly with some of the butter. Repeat with 5 of the remaining halved phyllo sheets and some of the remaining butter. Sprinkle with all but 1 tbsp of the walnuts; top with pear mixture. Arrange 1 halved phyllo sheet over top; brush lightly with some of the remaining butter. Repeat with remaining phyllo sheets and butter.

Using sharp knife, cut through layers to make 9 squares; halve squares diagonally to make 18 triangles. Bake in 350°F oven until phyllo is golden and pears are tender, about 45 minutes.

While baklava is baking, in saucepan, cook sugar, fresh ginger, cinnamon sticks, cloves and ⅓ cup water over medium-high heat, stirring, until sugar isdissolved; bring to boil. Reduce heat and simmer until syrupy, about 6 minutes. Remove from heat; stir in orange zest and lemon juice. Let stand until slightly thickened, about 15 minutes. Strain through fine-mesh sieve; discard solids. Pour over hot baklava; sprinkle with remaining walnuts. Let cool completely in pan, about 1 hour.

NUTRITIONAL INFORMATION PER PIECE about 134 cal, 2 g pro, 6 g total fat (2 g sat. fat), 19 g carb (1 g dietary fibre, 11 g sugar), 7 mg chol, 63 mg sodium, 60 mg potassium. % RDI: 1% calcium, 4% iron, 2% vit A, 2% vit C, 6% folate.

MAKES 6 TARTS
HANDS-ON TIME 15 MINUTES
TOTAL TIME 50 MINUTES

Honey, Fig & Mascarpone Tarts

1	sheet (half 450 g pkg) frozen butter puff pastry, thawed
2	egg yolks
½ cup	mascarpone cheese
3 tbsp	granulated sugar
4	Mission figs, cut in ½-inch thick wedges
2 tbsp	pistachios, toasted and coarsely chopped
2 tsp	liquid wildflower honey
2 tsp	lemon juice

On work surface, gently unroll pastry. Halve pastry lengthwise; cut crosswise into thirds to make 6 rectangles. Arrange, 2 inches apart, on parchment paper–lined rimless baking sheet.

Using sharp knife, score along border of each rectangle, ½ inch from edges. Whisk 1 of the egg yolks with 1 tsp water; lightly brush over edges of pastry.

In bowl, stir together mascarpone, sugar and remaining egg yolk; spoon generous 1 tbsp into centre of each rectangle, spreading to scored edges. Arrange figs over top. Bake in 400°F oven until edges are golden, about 16 minutes. Sprinkle with pistachios. Let cool to room temperature, about 20 minutes.

Whisk honey with lemon juice; drizzle over tarts.

NUTRITIONAL INFORMATION PER TART about 290 cal, 6 g pro, 18 g total fat (10 g sat. fat), 26 g carb (2 g dietary fibre, 10 g sugar), 78 mg chol, 138 mg sodium, 79 mg potassium. % RDI: 5% calcium, 9% iron, 10% vit A, 2% vit C, 5% folate.

TIP FROM THE TEST KITCHEN

To choose figs that are perfectly ripe, check that they're slightly soft to the touch.

Lemon Amaretto Tiramisu

MAKES 16 TO 20 SERVINGS
HANDS-ON TIME 1 HOUR
TOTAL TIME 13½ HOURS

1½ cups	sliced natural (skin-on) almonds
1	egg white
2 cups	granulated sugar
12	egg yolks
4 tsp	grated lemon zest
1 cup	lemon juice
1 cup	cold butter, cubed
⅓ cup	amaretto liqueur
18	ladyfingers (about 4 inches long)
1	tub (475 g) mascarpone cheese
2 cups	icing sugar
1 tsp	vanilla
2½ cups	whipping cream (35%)

Toss almonds with egg white to coat; stir in ¼ cup of the granulated sugar until well combined. Spread on parchment paper–lined rimmed baking sheet. Bake in 350°F oven, stirring once, until light golden, about 12 minutes. Let cool on sheet. *(Make-ahead: Store in airtight container for up to 2 days.)*

While almonds are baking, in large heatproof bowl, whisk together egg yolks, 1½ cups of the granulated sugar, the lemon zest and lemon juice. Place bowl over saucepan of simmering water; cook, stirring, until thick enough to coat back of spoon, about 12 minutes. Remove from heat; stir in butter, 1 tbsp at a time. Strain through fine-mesh sieve into clean bowl. Place plastic wrap directly on surface of curd. Refrigerate until curd is thick enough to mound firmly on spoon, about 1 hour. *(Make-ahead: Refrigerate for up to 2 days.)*

While lemon curd is chilling, in saucepan, cook remaining granulated sugar with ¼ cup water over medium heat, stirring, until sugar is dissolved. Remove from heat; let cool completely. Stir in amaretto. Quickly dip both sides of ladyfingers in amaretto mixture; arrange in single layer in 13- x 9-inch baking dish.

In large bowl, beat together mascarpone, icing sugar and vanilla until smooth. In separate bowl, beat 1½ cups of the cream until stiff peaks form; fold into mascarpone mixture. Spoon mixture over ladyfingers, spreading to edges. Spread lemon curd evenly over top. Cover and refrigerate for 12 hours. *(Make-ahead: Refrigerate for up to 24 hours. Let stand at room temperature for 10 minutes before continuing with recipe.)*

In bowl, beat remaining cream until stiff peaks form. Spoon over lemon curd, leaving border of curd. Sprinkle with almonds.

NUTRITIONAL INFORMATION PER EACH OF 20 SERVINGS about 535 cal, 8 g pro, 37 g total fat (20 g sat. fat), 44 g carb (1 g dietary fibre, 36 g sugar), 222 mg chol, 121 mg sodium, 143 mg potassium. % RDI: 11% calcium, 9% iron, 32% vit A, 10% vit C, 14% folate.

MAKES ABOUT 30 COOKIES
HANDS-ON TIME 30 MINUTES
TOTAL TIME 2½ HOURS

Chocolate Ginger Biscotti

BISCOTTI

½ cup	butter, softened
1 cup	granulated sugar
2	large eggs
1½ tsp	grated orange zest
1 tsp	vanilla
2½ cups	all-purpose flour
2 tsp	baking powder
¼ tsp	salt
170 g	dark chocolate (about 6 oz), chopped
⅓ cup	chopped crystallized ginger
1	egg white

COATING

140 g	dark chocolate (about 5 oz), melted

BISCOTTI In large bowl, beat butter with sugar until fluffy; beat in eggs, 1 at a time. Beat in orange zest and vanilla. In separate bowl, whisk together flour, baking powder and salt; stir into butter mixture in 2 additions just until combined. Stir in chocolate and ginger.

Divide dough in half. On lightly floured work surface, shape each half into 12-inch long log. Arrange, 2 inches apart, on parchment paper–lined rimless baking sheet; press to flatten slightly. Whisk egg white with 1 tsp water; brush generously over tops of logs. Bake in 325°F oven until light golden and firm to the touch, about 35 minutes. Let cool on pan for 10 minutes.

Transfer logs to cutting board. Using sharp chef's knife, cut diagonally into ½-inch thick slices. Stand slices upright, about ½ inch apart, on baking sheet. Bake in 300°F oven until almost dry, about 35 minutes. Transfer directly to racks to cool completely.

COATING Dip 1 end of each biscotti into chocolate, letting excess drip off. Place on waxed paper–lined baking sheet. Refrigerate until chocolate is set, about 20 minutes. *(Make-ahead: Layer between waxed paper in airtight container; store for up to 5 days or freeze for up to 2 weeks.)*

NUTRITIONAL INFORMATION PER COOKIE about 159 cal, 2 g pro, 7 g total fat (4 g sat. fat), 21 g carb (1 g dietary fibre, 12 g sugar), 22 mg chol, 69 mg sodium, 94 mg potassium. % RDI: 2% calcium, 10% iron, 3% vit A, 8% folate.

Cassis & Strawberry Labneh Clouds

MAKES 4 SERVINGS
HANDS-ON TIME 25 MINUTES
TOTAL TIME 1¼ HOURS

4 cups	hulled strawberries, quartered
1 cup	granulated sugar
1 cup	crème de cassis
2 cups	labneh or Greek yogurt
⅓ cup	chopped toasted salted pistachios

In large bowl, toss together strawberries, sugar and crème de cassis. Let stand until mixture is syrupy, 20 minutes to 1 hour.

Strain strawberry syrup into large saucepan. Return strawberries to same bowl. Bring strawberry syrup to boil over medium-high heat; cook until thick, 10 to 15 minutes. Scrape into small bowl; stir in 1 tbsp water. Let cool to room temperature. If syrup becomes too thick, gently warm in saucepan and stir in up to 1 tbsp hot water to thin. Divide labneh among 4 bowls.

Divide half of the strawberry syrup among bowls, swirling into labneh. Top with strawberries; sprinkle with pistachios. Drizzle with remaining syrup, if desired.

NUTRITIONAL INFORMATION PER SERVING about 484 cal, 15 g pro, 18 g total fat (9 g sat. fat), 63 g carb (5 g dietary fibre, 52 g sugar), 50 mg chol, 368 mg sodium, 376 mg potassium. % RDI: 6% calcium, 9% iron, 17% vit A, 115% vit C, 11% folate.

TIP FROM THE TEST KITCHEN

Labneh is a thick, velvety strained yogurt with a mascarpone-like flavour, available in Middle Eastern grocery stores and specialty shops. To make your own, line a fine-mesh sieve with cheesecloth or a large coffee filter; set over a large bowl. Spoon in Greek yogurt; refrigerate and let drain overnight.

MAKES 8 TO 10 SERVINGS
HANDS-ON TIME 25 MINUTES
TOTAL TIME 2 HOURS

Apple & Honey Challah Cake

10 cups cubed challah, cut in ½-inch pieces
4 McIntosh apples, peeled, cored and thinly sliced
1 tsp cinnamon
5 large eggs
⅓ cup liquid honey
2½ cups almond milk
½ cup canola or sunflower oil
1 tbsp vanilla
½ tsp salt
1 cup fig jam (approx)
½ cup sliced almonds
8 fresh Mission figs, halved lengthwise
2 tsp icing sugar

Arrange challah in single layer on 2 rimmed baking sheets; toast in 350°F oven until golden, 8 to 10 minutes.

Meanwhile, grease bottom of 8- or 9-inch springform pan; line side with parchment paper. Place pan on large square of heavy-duty foil; press foil up onto side of pan.

In large bowl, toss apples with cinnamon; set aside. In separate large bowl, whisk eggs with honey until combined. Whisk in almond milk, oil, vanilla and salt.

Toss together one-third each of challah and apple mixture with one-third of egg mixture. Transfer to prepared springform pan, pressing firmly to fill any holes. Dollop ½ cup of the jam by the spoonful over top. For second layer, toss together one-third each of challah and apple mixture with one-third of egg mixture. Transfer mixture to pan; top with remaining jam. Toss together remaining challah and apple mixture with remaining egg mixture; add to pan, pressing firmly.

Top with almonds. Let stand for 30 minutes at room temperature.

Set springform pan on rimmed baking sheet; bake in 350°F oven until challah is golden and puffed and custard is set, about 1 hour. Let cool for 15 minutes before unmoulding. Top with figs and dust with icing sugar.

NUTRITIONAL INFORMATION PER EACH OF 10 SERVINGS about 567 cal, 12 g pro, 22 g total fat (3 g sat. fat), 83 g carb (5 g dietary fibre, 36 g sugar), 132 mg chol, 550 mg sodium, 374 mg potassium. % RDI: 15% calcium, 24% iron, 20% vit A, 8% vit C, 36% folate.

Nutrition Information

To meet nutrient needs each day, moderately active women aged 25 to 49 need about 1,900 calories, 51 g protein, 261 g carbohydrate, 25 to 35 g fibre and not more than 63 g total fat (21 g saturated fat). Men and teenagers usually need more. Canadian sodium intake of approximately 3,500 mg daily should be reduced, whereas the intake of potassium from food sources should be increased to 4,700 mg per day. The percentage of recommended daily intake (% RDI) is based on the values used for Canadian food labels for calcium, iron, vitamins A and C, and folate.

Figures are rounded off. They are based on the first ingredient listed when there is a choice and do not include optional ingredients or those with no specified amounts.

Abbreviations

cal = calories **pro** = protein **carb** = carbohydrate **sat. fat** = saturated fat **chol** = cholesterol

Index

CONTRIBUTORS

RECIPES

All recipes were developed and Tested Till Perfect by the Canadian Living Test Kitchen

PHOTOGRAPHY

JEFF COULSON 13, 22, 39, 40, 45, 50, 77, 78, 86, 119, 124, 141

ANGUS FERGUSSON 8, 31, 97, 123

BROOKE LARK 4/5

JODI PUDGE 35, 49, 58, 71, 72, 85, 91, 92, 104, 132, 147, 148, 151

CHRISTINE SIRACUSA 159

ROBERTA SORGE 2

MARKUS SPISKE 152

RONALD TSANG 46, 114, 142

JAMES TSE 131

MAYA VISNYEI 14, 21, 29, 36, 57, 66, 103, 113

FOOD STYLING

BERNADETTE AMMAR 40

ASHLEY DENTON 58, 72, 104, 147, 148

MICHAEL ELLIOTT 14, 57, 97, 113, 123

DAVID GRENIER 13, 21, 22, 29, 35, 45, 46, 49, 50, 71, 85, 91, 92, 103, 119, 124, 142, 151

MIRANDA KEYES 77

LUCIE RICHARD 131

CHRISTOPHER ST. ONGE 8, 86, 114, 120

CLAIRE STUBBS 36, 39, 66, 132

NICOLE YOUNG 141

PROP STYLING

LAURA BRANSON 71, 77, 85, 92, 131, 132

AURALIE BRYCE 114

CATHERINE DOHERTY 8, 13, 21, 29, 45, 46, 49, 58, 72, 97, 103, 142, 148

JENNIFER EVANS 14, 57, 104, 113

ANN MARIE FAVOT 151

MADELEINE JOHARI 39, 114, 123, 141, 147

SABRINA LINN 22

ANDREA MCCRINDLE 35, 91

LARA MCGRAW 35

SASHA SEYMOUR 40, 86, 120

CAROLYN SOUCH 50, 124

PAIGE WEIR 66